# Primary Partners
### "Faith in God"

# We Love
# Activity Days
### for Girls, Ages 8-11

## 30 Goal Activities With:
**Invitations**
**Goal Activities**
**Success Snacks**

## 5 Planners to Prepare Age-11 Girls for Young Women

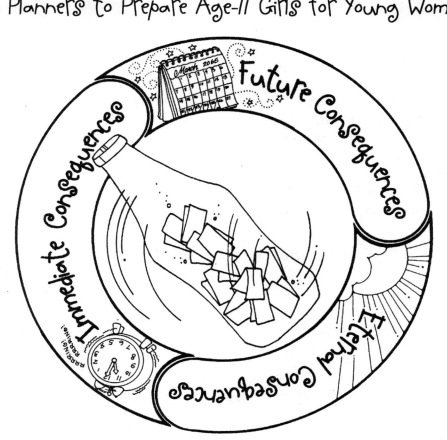

# Introducing the Author and Illustrator, Creators of the Following Series of Books and CD-ROMS:

*Primary Partners*® (lesson match activities)*: Nursery 1 & 2, CTR A, CTR B, Old Testament, New Testament, Book of Mormon, Doctrine & Covenants; Primary Partners*®*: Sharing Time, Sharing Time Teaching Treasures, Singing Fun, "Faith in God" Activity Days; Young Women: Young Women Fun-tastic! Activities for Manual 1; Manual 2; Manual 3,* and *Young Women Fun-tastic! Personal Progress Motivators.* FHE & Primary: *Gospel Fun Activities, Gospel Games, Super Singing Activities, Super Little Singers, File-Folder Family Home Evenings,* and *Home-spun Fun Family Home Evenings*

**Mary Ross, Author**

Mary Ross is an energetic mother and has been a Primary, Young Women, and Relief Society teacher and leader. She loves to help children and young women have a good time while learning. She has studied acting, modeling, and voice. Her varied interests include writing, creating activities and children's parties, and cooking. Mary and her husband, Paul, live with their daughter, Jennifer, in Sandy, Utah.

**Jennette Guymon-King, Illustrator**

Jennette Guymon-King studied graphic arts and illustration at Utah Valley College and the University of Utah. She served a mission in Japan. Jennette enjoys sports, reading, cooking, art, gardening, and freelance illustrating. Jennette and her husband, Clayton, live in Riverton, Utah. They are the proud parents of their daughter Kayla Mae, and sons Levi and Carson.

Copyright © 2003 by Mary H. Ross and Jennette Guymon-King
All Rights Reserved
Covenant Communications, Inc.
American Fork, Utah

Printed in United States of America
First Printing: September 2003

*Primary Partners*® *"Faith in God" We Love Activity Days*
ISBN 1-59156-343-7

Acknowledgments: Thanks to Inspire Graphics ( www.inspiregraphics.com) for Lettering Delights computer fonts. —This product is neither sponsored nor endorsed by The Church of Jesus Christ of Latter-day Saints.

# INTRODUCTION

### *We Love Activity Days* Will Help Girls Ages 8-11 Achieve
### "Faith in God" Goals in the Following Areas:

- Learning and Living the Gospel
- Developing Talents
- Serving Others
- Preparing for Young Women

With this volume of *Primary Partners* Activity Days, every detail is worked out for you, allowing you to concentrate on the different personalities and needs of each girl. You will find activities to help girls achieve each goal in the "Faith in God" Program.

## For Each "Faith in God" Goal You Will Find:

- An invitation to encourage girls to attend the activity (sample shown right).
- Motivating activities for each goal. Simply copy* and cut out the goal instructions and visuals for each girl. Goal instructions are found below each invitation (sample below). Each activity is designed to help girls achieve the goal in a fun, entertaining way.
- A Thought Treat for each activity can be found at the end of each section.
- Plus, you will find planner forms and an invitation to a special activity to help age 11 girls prepare for Young Women.

## Easy Ways to Help Girls Love Activity Days:

1. *Choose Goals:* Have girls select the goals they wish to work on for the year and plan the group activities accordingly.

2. *Have Girls Help Plan Activities:* There are no instructions in this book for the leaders, so you will need to follow the goal instructions that follow each invitation, e.g., the *Serving Others Goal 1* activity (shown right).

3. *Gather Supplies Ahead of Time.*

4. *Help Girls Stay Caught Up:* If girls miss an activity, simply give them their goal instructions and visuals to work on at home with a friend or parent. This makes it super easy for the leaders.

5. *Enjoy Thought Treats:* Girls can take turns preparing these. Simply copy the ideas following each section, cut out instructions and delegate.

*__*Quick-and-Easy Plan:__* Print all of the activities and patterns in this book in color or black and white, using the *Primary Partners "Faith in God": We Love Activity Days* CD-ROM (shown right). Also see samples on the back cover of this book.

Serving Others  Goal 1  Samaritan Service: Service Helps My Faith Grow Stronger

**ACTIVITY 1:** *Read and discuss the parable of the good Samaritan (see Luke 10:30-37).*
Discussion:
Talk about how the good Samaritan gave of his time, talent, and means to help someone in need.

**ACTIVITY 2:** *Plan and complete a service project that helps a family member or neighbor.*
Good Samaritan (Secret Service Project)
1. Obtain and color the *Good Samaritan Secret Service Project* planner (shown right).
2. To plan your service project, answer the questions on the planner, e.g., "who," "what," etc. to plan your service project.
3. Assign certain girls certain tasks on the planner. Then complete service project in secret(showing anonymous service) if possible.

**ACTIVITY 3:** *After completing the project, discuss how it helped your faith grow stronger and record it on the planner.*

GOOD SAMARITAN SECRET SERVICE PROJECT
WHO WE WANT TO SERVE:
WHAT WE WANT TO DO:
WHERE WE WILL GO:
WHEN WE WILL SERVE:
WHY WE WANT TO SERVE:
MY ASSIGNMENT:
COMPLETE AFTER PROJECT: HOW DID THIS PROJECT HELP MY FAITH GROW STRONGER?

# TABLE OF CONTENTS

### Activities to Help Girls Achieve "Faith in God" Goals :

### Learning and Living the Gospel:

# Serving Others:

# Developing Talents:

# Preparing for Young Women (Girls, Age 11):

1—Seek Uplifting and Virtuous Things
2—The Purpose and Importance of the Young Women Program
3—Ideas on Serving the Lord and Stranding for Truth and Righteousness
4—Education Strengths
5—Strengthening My Family

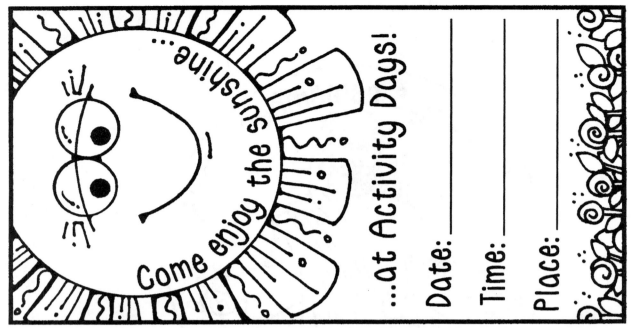

**...at Activity Days!**

Date: _____

Time: _____

Place: _____

Learning & Living the Gospel   Goal 1

Covenants: I Will Remain Faithful

**ACTIVITY 1:** *Explain how taking the sacrament helps you renew your baptismal covenant.*

### Sunshine Promises (Mirror Motivator)

1. Obtain and color the *Sunshine Promises Mirror Motivator* (shown right).

2. Place the sun/Jesus picture on your mirror and write on each sun ray what you will do to keep this baptismal covenant. Example: On the "Stand as a Witness" sun ray you might write, "I will bear my testimony." Put a different sun ray up every two days and work on it, completing the five sun rays in the next two weeks.

3. Read the sacrament prayer in D&C 20: 77, 79. Talk about the promise we make while we take the sacrament: "I will always remember Him." This promise is found on the *Sunshine Promises Mirror Motivator*.

**ACTIVITY 2:** *In a family home evening, teach others about things we can do to remain faithful.*

### Faithful Footsteps Game (Family Home Evening Activity)

1. Obtain and color the *Faithful Footsteps Game Family Home Evening Activity* situations and obtain a spoon for every player. Cut up the situations and place them in a container.

2. Read about covenants and promises in Mosiah 5:2, 5, and Mosiah 18:7-17.

3. Play the Faithful Footsteps Game (shown right).

*How to Play:* (1) Sit in a circle with a spoon for every player, taking away one spoon to start. (2) Have someone draw a situation and call it out. If the action is something faithful, everyone grabs a spoon. The person without a spoon goes out, taking a spoon with them. (3) Keep playing until you find a winner. The winner is the one who grabs the last spoon. Play again and again until all situations are read. If you run out of situations before the game ends, refer to previously read situations again until the game ends.

I will always remember Jesus.

## Keep the Commandments

I will _____
_____
_____
_____

## Mourn With Those That Mourn

I will _____
_____
_____
_____

Comfort Those
That Need Comfort

I will ____

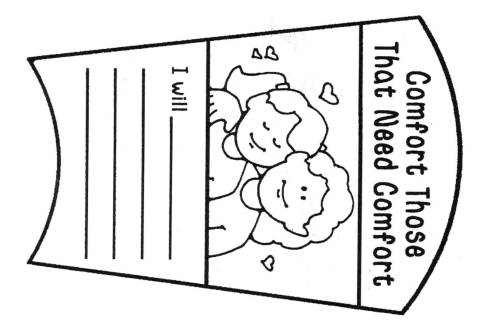

Bear One
Another's Burdens

I will ____

Stand As
a Witness

I will ____

| | |
|---|---|
| I prayed every night, but prayed the same prayer. | Drugs at school are available, but I say no. |
| I went shopping on the Sabbath because my brother was sick and I had to get his medicine. While I was there I bought my favorite candy bar. | I told my parents I would tend my sister while they went to the temple, but I stayed at my friend's house too long, so my parents couldn't go. |
| I felt like kicking my big brother for eating my pie, but I didn't. | It would be so easy to do drugs, smoke, or drink alcohol, but I remember that my body needs to last. |
| I remembered the 12th Article of Faith about honoring the law, but I stole some candy any way. | I listened to my mother as she asked me to empty the garbage, but I played the piano instead. |
| I took the sacrament on Sunday but I had a guilty conscience because I was mean to my sister and did not repent. | I wish that my sister and I got along better, but I just can't forgive her for embarrassing me in front of my friends. |
| I thought about listening to general conference on Saturday, but played with my friends instead. | I really respect the girls at school who dress modestly, so I try to do the same. |
| I memorized a scripture that said to be a light, but I was a poor example to my friend. | There are so many programs on television that are not pleasing to Heavenly Father, so I turn them off. |
| I wanted to kick my dog, but chose to feed and take care of him instead. | I like to listen to music that gives me peace and helps me feel the Spirit. |
| My friend was confused about something she read in the Bible, so I went to Joseph Smith's Translation in Matthew to find the answer. | When I find myself in a friendship where the friend chooses the do the wrong and asks me to do so, I usually end the friendship and tell them why. |
| I believe in personal revelation, but sometimes I forget to pray to know what I should do. | I want to treat everyone kindly, but when people try to push bad things on me, I don't want to hurt their feelings, but I say "no" anyway. |
| I seek after things that are of "good report," like the 13th Article of Faith says, but I don't work hard in school to get a good report card. | I hear gossip about some girls at school. I don't like this and try not to repeat what I hear. |
| My friend and I like to listen to music and we play one song over and over, even though it encourages low morals. | I try to seek good friends, even those who are not popular at school. I guess I just feel good being around people who have good standards. |
| I want to follow Heavenly Father's plan for me, so I attend church every Sunday. | I want to be worthy to go to the temple someday, but for now I wear shorter skirts, shorts, and shirts than I should. |

| | |
|---|---|
| I listen to the Holy Ghost, but sometimes I don't obey His voice and feel sorrow. | I went to a party and everything was fun, even though we watched an R rated movie. |
| I know that if I choose the right I can repent. But sometimes I keep on making wrong choices because I know I have already messed up. | I want to serve a mission someday, but I forget to read my scriptures at night, so I'm not sure if I'll be ready. |
| I made a nice card for my grandmother, but I never sent it. | I want to have a strong body and be able to run without being weary, but I eat junk food. |
| I told my friend I couldn't help him, but changed my mind. | I didn't volunteer to help my sister dry the dishes, but I dried them anyway. |
| It was late and I still wasn't home. I wanted to call my mother to let her know, but I didn't. | I can't remember the last time I called my grandmother to see how she is. |
| I told my father I would put air in his bike tire, but forgot. When he hurried out to ride it, the tire was flat. | I told the missionaries I didn't know anyone who wanted to hear the gospel, but I thought about it and gave them a name of my friend. |
| The scriptures say not to hide my light under a bushel. I didn't choose the right and dimmed my light. | My grandmother asked me to do something and paid me to do it. I accepted the money, but didn't do as she asked. |
| My friend asked me to skip school, and I said, "No, it's not cool!" | I said I would help with family home evening, but got sick. I said, "Sorry." |
| I read about Nephi's courage, but I doubted that I could do it, so I didn't even try. | I decided to tell my sick friend about a special assignment at school. I went towards his house but met another friend and forgot. |
| When it's Christmas time I am tempted to buy gifts for myself, but I buy for others instead. | Tomorrow is the last day for a book report but I didn't read my book. My friend offered to give me her notes, but I stayed up all night and read instead. |
| I stopped to help a friend, but changed my mind. | I volunteered to give a talk in Primary and worked on it all week. I gave a great talk. |
| I told my mother I would be home early, but I forgot and came home late. | I promised to help when there was work to do. Then I forgot and didn't pull through. |
| I told my mother I would watch my little brother, but he got lost. | My friend who is of another faith asked me about Activity Days and Primary, so I asked her if she wanted to go. |
| I rushed off to school to find out that I was wearing two different shoes, but I went to class and listened anyway. | I looked under the table and found the $10 bill that Dad lost. I needed the money, but I didn't delay; I gave him the money anyway. |
| I didn't want to go to church because my hair looked dorky, but I went anyway. | I told a joke to cheer up a friend, but the joke was a dirty joke. |

## Learning & Living the Gospel  Goal 2

"If any of you lack wisdom, let him ask of God, that giveth to all men liberally, and upbraideth not and it shall be given him." —James 1:5

### Prayer: I Will Pray Sincerely

**ACTIVITY 1:** *Give a family home evening on Joseph Smith's First Vision (see Joseph Smith—1:1-20).*

### First Vision (Family Home Evening)

Obtain and color the *First Vision Stand-Up Figures* (shown left) in order to make this presentation telling the story from the scriptures. See Joseph Smith—History 1:1-20.

**ACTIVITY 2:** *Discuss how Heavenly Father answers our sincere prayers.*

### Puzzled About Prayer (Match Game)

Jenny prayed about going to a party with her new friend.

She didn't have a good feeling about going.

Nicky prayed to find friends.

When she met Angie she had a warm feeling.

Nicole prayed that she would get some clothes and shoes she really needed.

A neighbor felt inspired to give her the clothes her daughter didn't need.

Sarah fell and twisted her ankle skating. It was getting dark and she prayed for help.

She felt comforted and knew that her father would come looking for her.

Obtain, color, and cut out the *Puzzled About Prayer* cards (shown right).

**To Play:** Mix up the cards and place them facedown. Divide into teams and take turns turning two pieces over to make a match. Read the card and talk about how Heavenly Father answered the prayer.

**Ideas About Prayer:** Heavenly Father answers prayers in the impressions we feel or He inspires others to help us.  Our feelings might be one of these:
1. TO WAIT (a hesitant feeling)  2. GO AHEAD (a warm feeling)
3. DON'T GO AHEAD (a doubtful feeling).  Answers to prayers come if we listen, if we are worthy to receive the inspiration, and if our prayers are sincere.

"If any of you lack wisdom, let him ask of God, that giveth to all men liberally, and upbraideth not and it shall be given him."

-James 1:5

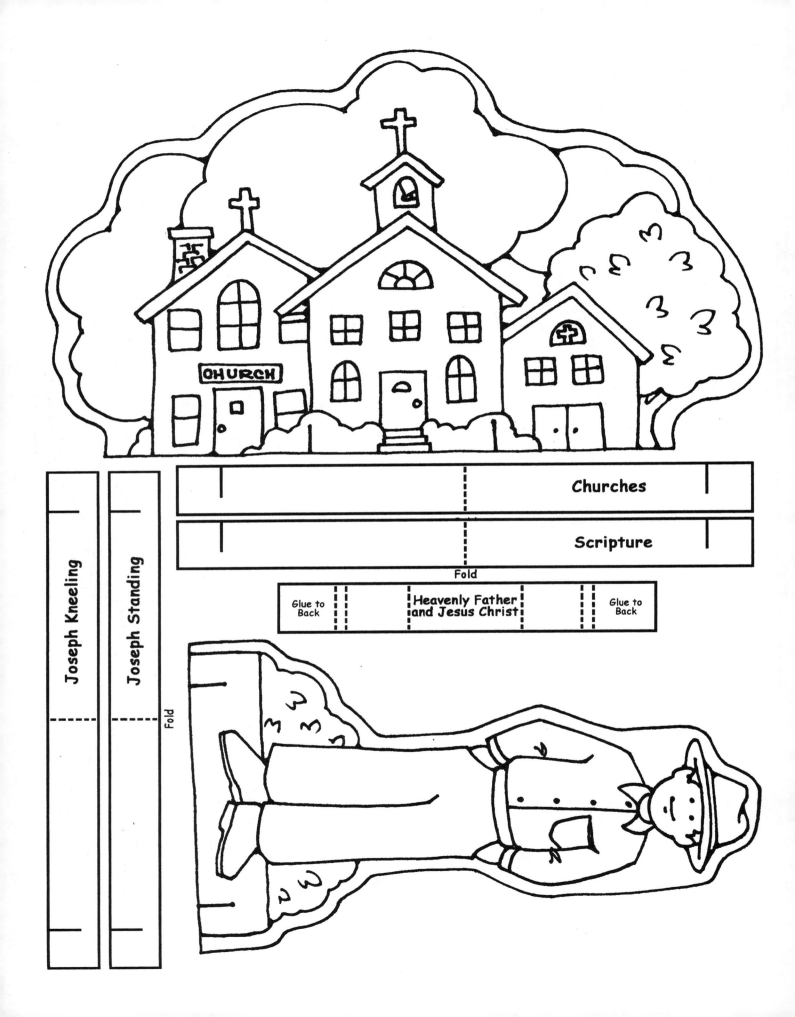

Churches

Scripture

Fold

Glue to Back

Heavenly Father and Jesus Christ

Glue to Back

Joseph Kneeling

Joseph Standing

Fold

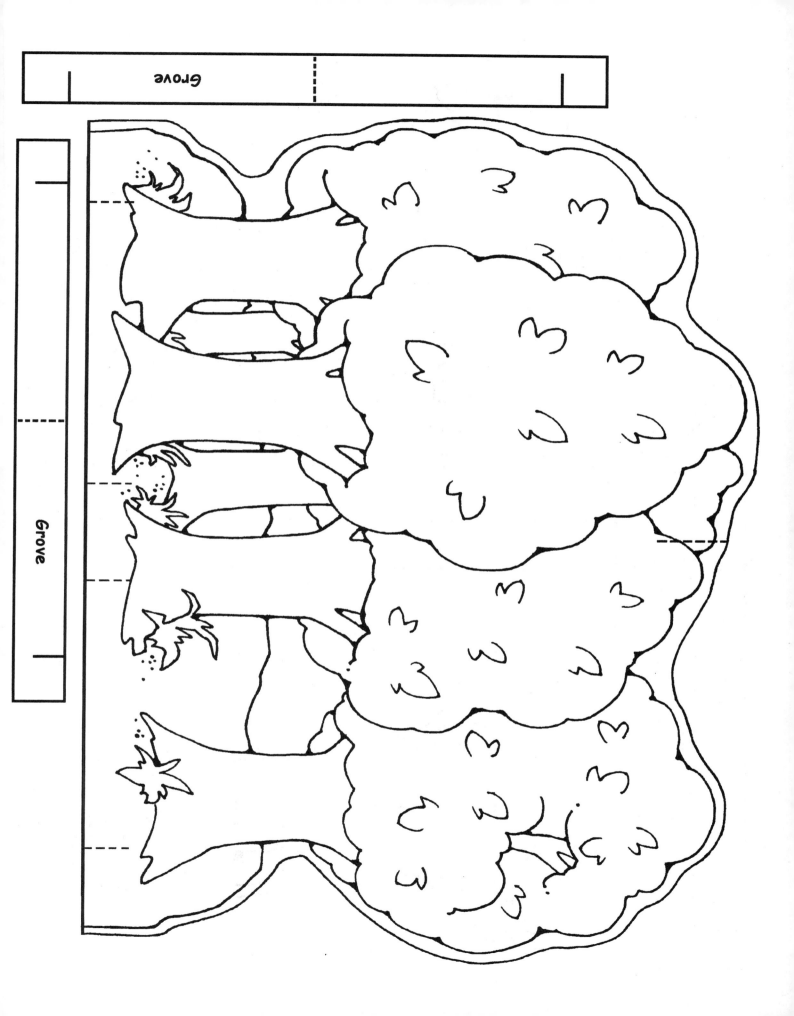

Grove

Grove

She felt impressed to look in her inside coat pocket.

McKenna lost her lunch money and prayed for help to find it.

She felt better and the angry feeling left.

Karen was angry at her friend and prayed for help.

A nearby neighbor's name came to her mind.

Anna was tending and the baby got sick. She prayed for help.

She had a warm and a happy feeling.

Alexa prayed to know if the Book of Mormon was really true.

One morning she felt uneasy about walking.

Hanna always prayed to be safe when walking to school.

She felt she should stay right where she was and keep calling for them.

Hope got lost while hiking with her family and prayed to know what to do.

Jenny prayed about going to a party with her new friend.

She didn't have a good feeling about going.

Nicky prayed to find friends with good values.

When she met Angie she had a warm feeling.

Wendy, couldn't sleep and was feeling scared.

She prayed and she felt inspired to read her scriptures.

Nicole prayed that she would get some clothes and shoes she really needed.

A neighbor felt inspired to give her the clothes her daughter didn't need.

Jill's dog wandered off and was hit by a car.

She prayed, and even though she was still sad she felt comforted.

Sarah fell and twisted her ankle skating. It was getting dark and she prayed for help.

She felt comforted and knew that her father would come looking for her.

Cindy was heartbroken when her grandfather died. She prayed for comfort.

She felt a calm feeling even though she still missed her grandpa.

Madison wanted an expensive bicycle for her birthday and prayed for it every day.

Each time she prayed she felt like it wasn't the right time.

Satomi prayed for strength to say "no" if a class member asked her to steal.

She felt better and thought she could choose the right.

Mandy prayed about the talk she was to give in church.

She felt inspired to tell about an experience she had.

Abby prayed about inviting a friend of another faith to attend a Primary activity with her.

She had a warm feeling.

Elise was invited to go camping with her friend's family and prayed about going.

She didn't feel good about accepting the invitation.

We hope you'll find your way to Activity Days!

Date: _____

Time: _____

Place: _____

## Learning & Living the Gospel  Goal 3
## Holy Ghost: The Holy Ghost Will Help Me Throughout My Life

**ACTIVITY 1:** *Mark these verses about the Holy Ghost in your scriptures: John 14:16-17, 2 Nephi 32:5, and Moroni 10:5.*

### Scripture Underling Guide and Pencil Pocket

*To Make:* Obtain, color, and cut out the *Scripture Underlining Guide and Pencil Pocket* (shown right). Fold and glue *Guide* edges, leaving the top open to create a pocket. Enclose a red pencil in the pocket. *To Underline Scriptures:* Use the *Scripture Underlining Guide* as a straight edge, placing it under the lines you wish to underline. Store the pencil in the pocket. Use pencil to underline scriptures about the Holy Ghost, or to underline other scriptures that inspire you to heed His promptings.

**ACTIVITY 2:** *Discuss ways the Holy Ghost helps you.*

## Let the Spirit Guide (Flashlight—Tag & Block—Toss Game)

*To Make:* Obtain, color, and cut out the *Let the Spirit Guide* circles, situation cards, and block (shown right). Fold block, stuff with cotton, and glue tabs to hold. You'll need three flashlights (one for leader).

*To Play:* (1) Divide players into two teams seated across from each other in a circle. (2) Place circles in the center and situation cards facedown. Have a player from each team be ready to shine their flashlight on the circle. Darken the room so you can see the flashlight's beam on the circles.  If the room is dark, have the leader use a flashlight to read the situation card.

(3) Have teams take turns drawing a situation card and, without looking, hand it to the leader to read, e.g., "Abby was lost and didn't know her way home." (4) First play *Flashlight Tag* and then *Block Toss* as follows:

• *Flashlight Tag:* The player representing each team identifies one of the three circles:  Comforts, Guides, Testifies of Truth by flashing their flashlight on the circle. The team player to identify the correct answer earns a point for their team. You will need another leader or girl as the referee (who knows the answer) to see which team flashes their light on the circle first. If there is any question, toss a coin (heads gets the point).

• *Block Toss:* The person who earns a point for their team can earn an extra point by tossing the block in the center. If it lands on the correct answer that was previously spotted, they earn an extra point for their team. Play until all the cards are read. The team with the most points wins!

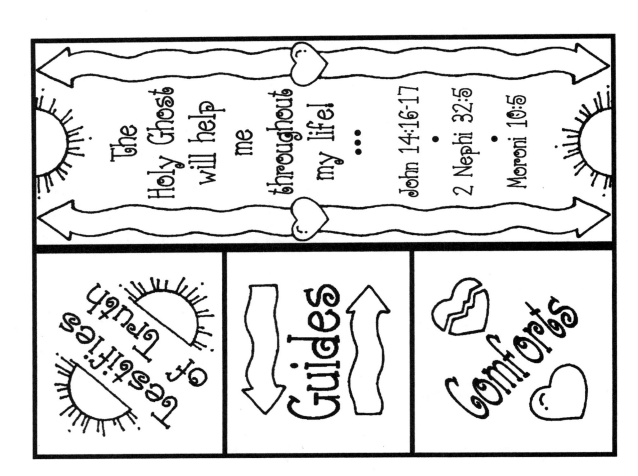

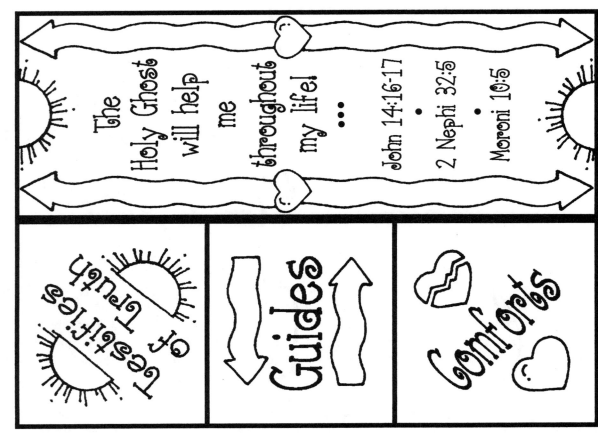

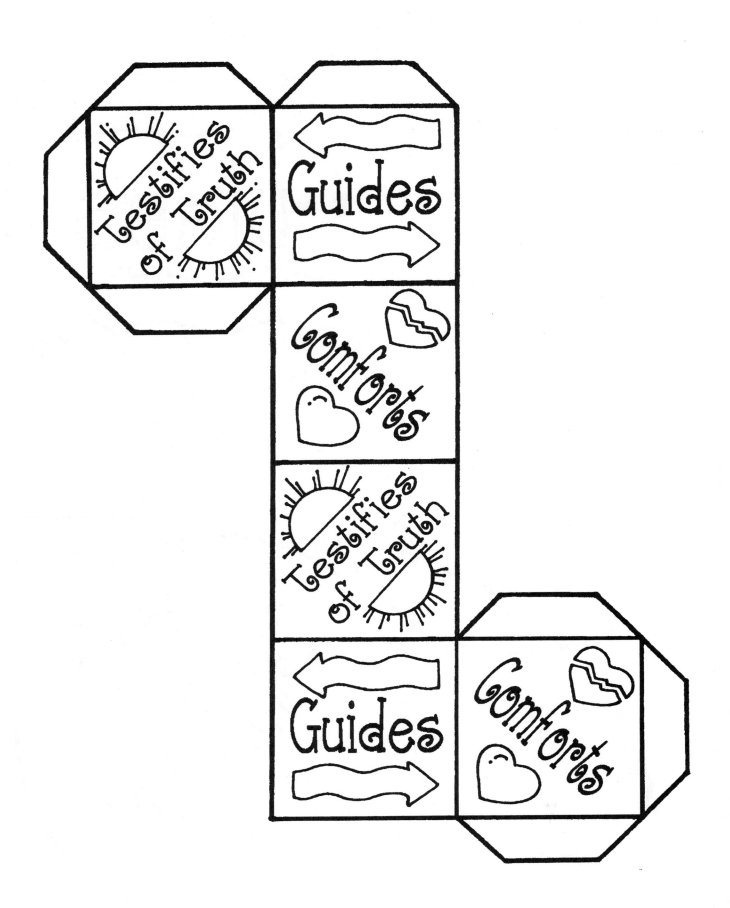

Abby was lost and didn't know her way home.          GUIDES

Seth's saw several bees in their house and wondered if there was a beehive inside.     GUIDES

Cindy was investigating the Church.
          TESTIFIES OF TRUTH

Bret's friends asked him to do something he wasn't sure he should do.          GUIDES

Carson wanted to bear his testimony but didn't know what to say.          GUIDES

Cheryl felt sad because her grandmother died.  COMFORTS

Cole was curious about smoking and wondered if he should.
          GUIDES

Kara's friend asked her to go to a party and she couldn't decide.
          GUIDES

Heidi couldn't decide if she should stay home from church or go.          GUIDES

Heather didn't have a testimony of the Book of Mormon.
          TESTIFIES OF TRUTH

Nick wanted to know why it was important his parents were sealed in the temple.
          TESTIFIES OF TRUTH

Cary was alone at home and was afraid.          COMFORTS

Megan wanted to go waterskiing and her parents said they didn't feel right about it.
          GUIDES

While Mary was babysitting, her little sister wandered off.
          GUIDES

Cynthia was very hungry but she still had two hours to go before she could break her fast.
          COMFORTS

Tina was tempted to spend her tithing and didn't know if she should pay it.          GUIDES

Lisa was walking her brother's dog when it ran away.
          GUIDES

Shane was feeling sad and someone at school gave him some drugs.          GUIDES

Nina was fishing and her dad left to go after bait. He wasn't back yet and it was getting dark.          COMFORTS

James needed some money and didn't know where to get a job.
          GUIDES

Jenny went hiking with her cousin and they couldn't find their way back to camp.
          GUIDES

Kevin took his little brother to the mall. His brother was playing Hide-and-Seek and got lost.          GUIDES

Abby's friend told her a movie was good and another friend told her it was bad.    GUIDES

Jessica couldn't understand why it is against the Word of Wisdom to drink coffee.
          TESTIFIES OF TRUTH

Hanna was about to be baptized and wanted to know if it was the right thing to do.
          TESTIFIES OF TRUTH

Alex's friend couldn't sit by him at lunch that day and some bullies tried to take his lunch.
          COMFORTS

Laura's friend was looking on her paper while thy were taking a test. She didn't know what to do or say.     GUIDES

Lydia played hard to win the soccer game, but her friends were mean to her for not making a goal.     COMFORTS

Stacy listened carefully as the missionaries told her that she and her family could be together forever.
          TESTIFIES OF TRUTH

Patricia wanted to know if what her Primary teacher was telling her was true.
          TESTIFIES OF TRUTH

Michelle's cat Butterscotch ran away and she couldn't find it anywhere.          COMFORTS

## Learning & Living the Gospel   Goal 4

## Obedience: I Will Follow the Prophet

**ACTIVITY 1: *Read a recent conference address given by the prophet* (in the May or November *Ensign* magazine).**

### Prophet Ponder (Doorknob Hanger)

1. Obtain, color, and cut out the *Prophet Ponder Doorknob Hanger* (shown right).
2. Write what you will do to follow the prophet on the doorknob hanger after reading the conference address (detailed above).
3. Hang the *Prophet Ponder* on your bedroom or bathroom door as a reminder.

**ACTIVITY 2: *Decide what you can do to follow the prophet, and do it.***

### Prophet Ponder (Guessing Game)

Obtain, color, and cut out the *Prophet Ponder Guessing Game* cards (shown left). You'll need straight pins or safety pins.

***To Play:***

1. Pin a card on the back of each player so they can't see the gospel principle the prophet wants us to obey. This principle is underlined on the card.
2. Play 20 Questions to figure out what we can do to follow the prophet. The person you ask can only give yes or no answers.
3. If the person guesses they can help others until the time is up.
4. Have everyone sit in a circle and spotlight each individual by reading their card and talking about how we are blessed by obeying the prophet in this way.

I Will Follow the Prophet

I will follow the prophet
by doing the following:

_____

_____

_____

_____

_____

I Will Follow the Prophet

I will follow the prophet
by doing the following:

_____

_____

_____

_____

_____

Pay your
tithing.

Plant a garden.

Keep the
Word of Wisdom.

Find friends that
choose the right.

Believe in
Jesus Christ.

Read and study
the Book
of Mormon.

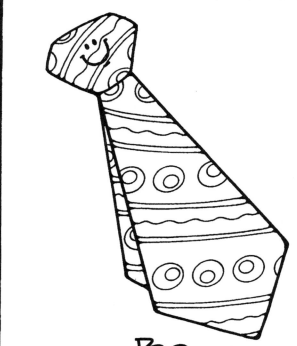

Be a
missionary.

Respect
your parents.

Write in
your journal
each day.

Be a friend to
the friendless.

Keep the
commandments.

Have family
home evening.

Strive to be worthy to attend the temple.

Attend your church meetings.

Love one another.

Keep the sabbath day holy.

Buzz on over...

...to Activity Days!

Date: _____

Time: _____

Place: _____

See you there!

Learning & Living the Gospel  Goal 5          Prayer: I Will Stay Close to Heavenly Father

**ACTIVITY 1:** *Give an opening and a closing prayer in family home evening or Primary.*
Check When Complete:  Opening Prayer ____  Closing Prayer ____

**ACTIVITY 2:** *Share your feelings about how prayer protects us and helps us to stay close to Heavenly Father and the Savior.*

### Prayer Blossoms (Board Game)

1. Obtain, color, and cut out the *Prayer Blossoms Board Game* block, game board, and bee markers (shown left).

2. Talk about how prayer with Heavenly Father helps your relationship blossom and grow—especially when the thorns of life come. If we pray daily and get close to Heavenly Father we will learn to depend on Him to protect and help us when we are in need.

3. Follow the rules on the game board to play the *Prayer Blossoms Board Game.*

← Cut carefully along the inside of the dotted line.

Go back 3 spaces.

you prayed. before (upside down)

Go to finish!

Don't forget to pray!

You pray with your family.

FINISH

Go back 1 space.

Your ♥ warmed when you prayed.

START

3 spaces.

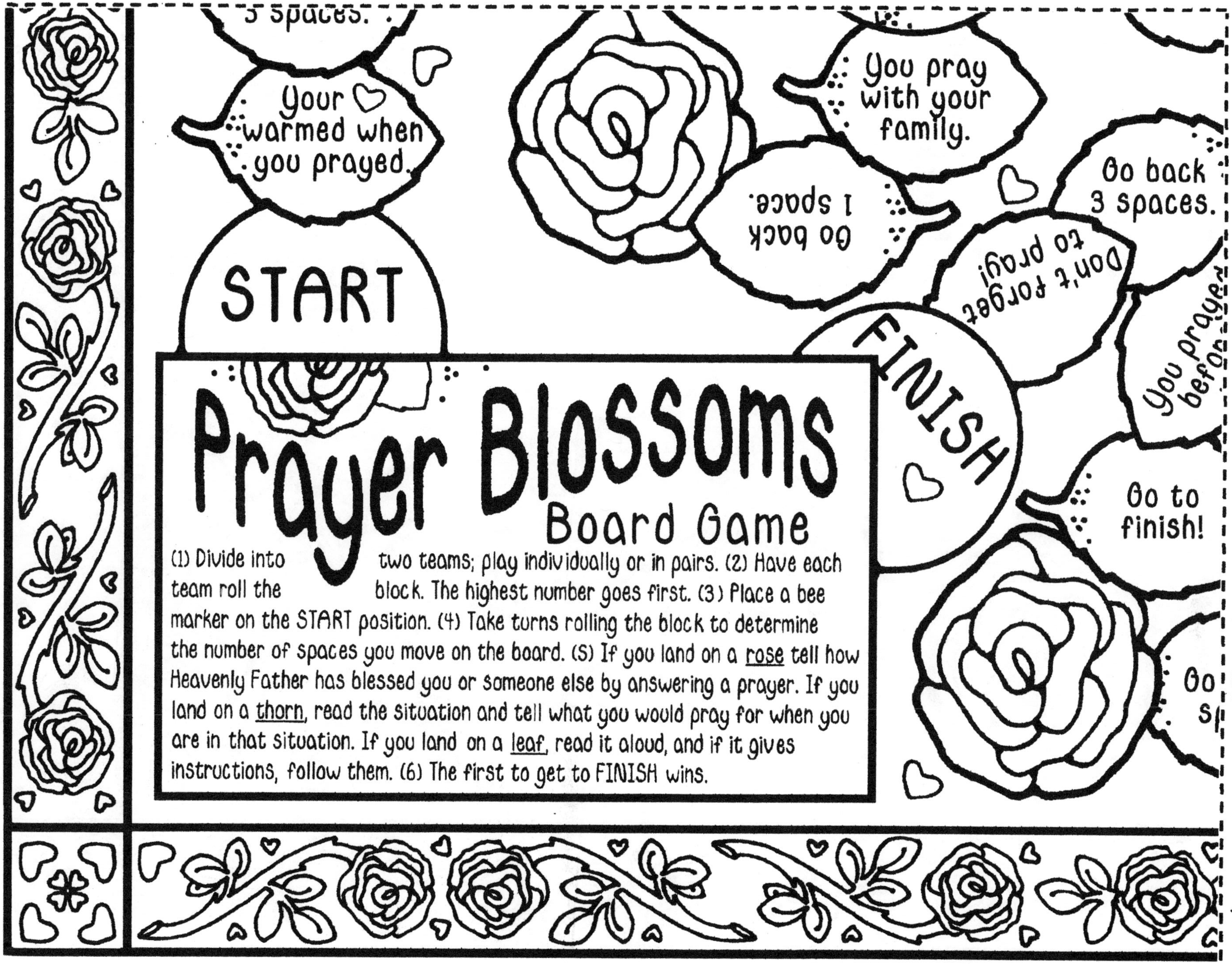

# Prayer Blossoms
## Board Game

(1) Divide into two teams; play individually or in pairs. (2) Have each team roll the block. The highest number goes first. (3) Place a bee marker on the START position. (4) Take turns rolling the block to determine the number of spaces you move on the board. (5) If you land on a <u>rose</u> tell how Heavenly Father has blessed you or someone else by answering a prayer. If you land on a <u>thorn</u>, read the situation and tell what you would pray for when you are in that situation. If you land on a <u>leaf</u>, read it aloud, and if it gives instructions, follow them. (6) The first to get to FINISH wins.

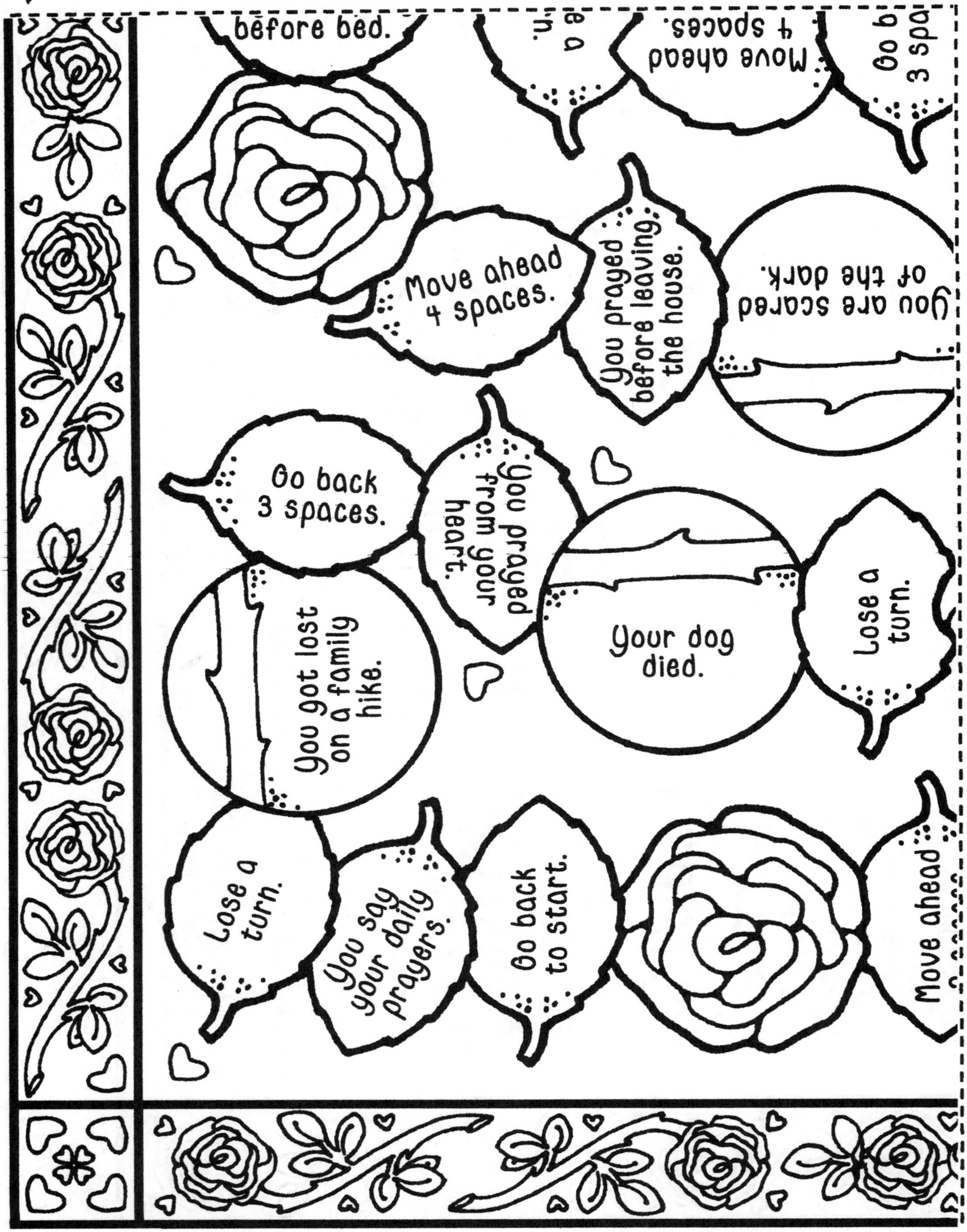

before bed.

Move ahead 4 spaces.

Go b 3 spa

Move ahead 4 spaces.

You prayed before leaving the house.

You are scared of the dark.

Go back 3 spaces.

You prayed from your heart.

Your dog died.

Lose a turn.

You got lost on a family hike.

Lose a turn.

You say your daily prayers.

Go back to start.

Move ahead

Do not cut along the dotted line. Use this margin to mount the other side.

You never forget to pray.

Move ahead 3 spaces.

Lose a turn

You have be very sick

Your father lost his job.

You pra when were s

Your brother needs an operation.

ve ahead spaces.

Go back 4 spaces.

You prayed before fasting.

You love your Heavenly Father.

you while hom to be

Lose a turn.

You forgot to pray. Go back 7 spaces.

Move ahead 7 spaces.

back 5 spaces.

test.

You prayed Just to say thank you.

come

Your house caught fire.

Move ahead 2 spaces.

prayed you Ad

You prayed to know what to do.

Your best friend moved away.

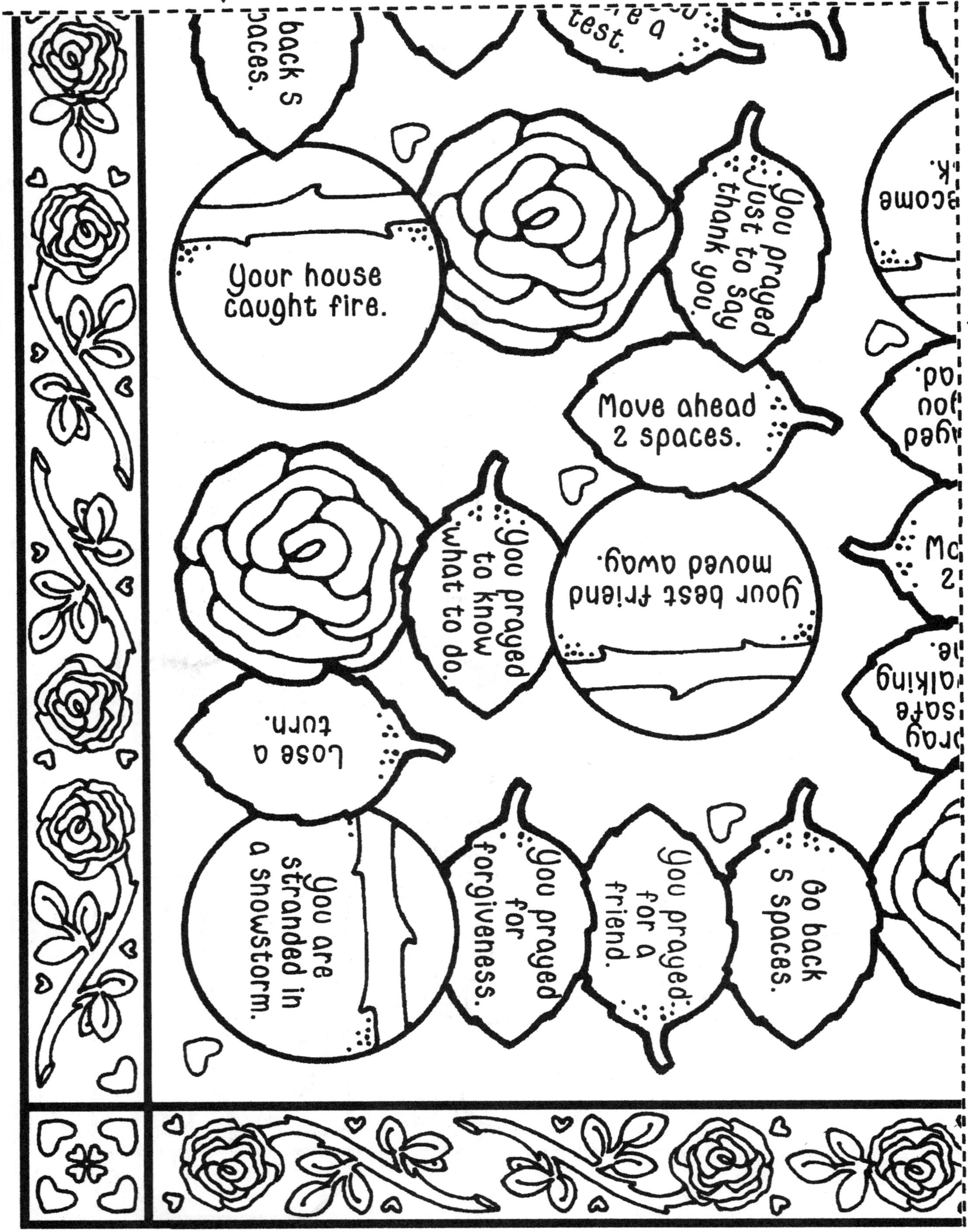

Mo 2

Lose a turn.

pray safe alking he

You are stranded in a snowstorm.

You prayed for forgiveness.

You prayed for a friend.

Go back 5 spaces.

Come enjoy
the treasures
on my pages...

...at Activity Days!

Date: _____

Time: _____

Place: _____

Bring your Book of Mormon.

## Learning & Living the Gospel  Goal 6

## Testimony: I Know Jesus Christ Lives

**ACTIVITY 1:** *Tell a story from the Book of Mormon that teaches about faith in Jesus Christ.*

### Book of Mormon Story—Abinidi Warns the Wicked King Noah (Puppet Show)

1. Obtain, color, and cut out the *Abinidi Warns the Wicked King Noah Puppet Show* (shown left).
2. Mount wooden craft sticks or tongue depressors on the bottom half (back) of each visual.
3. Put on the puppet show by having individuals hold the visuals while a narrator reads the script #1-14.

**ACTIVITY 2:** *Share your testimony of the Savior.*

### My Testimony of Jesus Christ (Journal Page)

1. Obtain, color, and cut out the *My Testimony of Jesus Christ Journal Page* (shown right).
2. Write your testimony of the Savior on the journal page. You might also want to express how 1) the gospel has blessed your life and 2) your belief that the Book of Mormon is true.
3. Place this in your own Book of Mormon. Also, you can place this same testimony in a Book of Mormon you can give away.

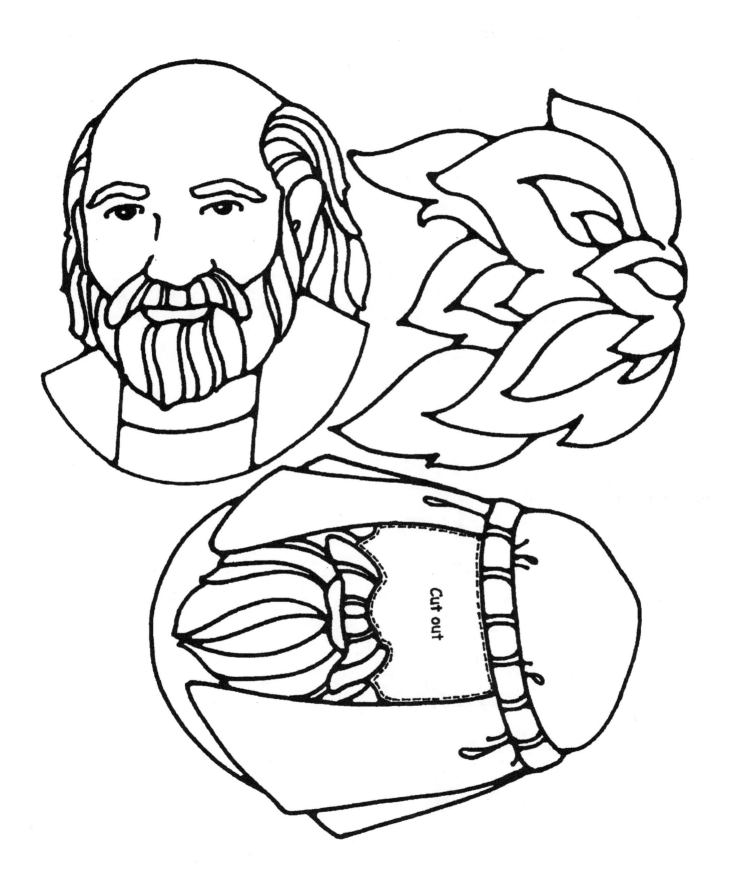

Cut out

# Book of Mormon Story: Abinadi Warns the Wicked King Noah and His Priests (Mosiah 11-19)

**1   King Noah:** Noah was not a good king like his father was. He was wicked and did not obey God's commandments. He forced the people to give of their grain, animals, gold, and silver so he would not have to work. He was lazy.

**2   Priests:** Noah's father had righteous priests. Noah replaced them with wicked priests who taught the people to sin. They liked to drink wine and enjoy the palace riches.

**3   Abinadi:** God sent a prophet named Abinadi to Noah's people. He warned them that if they did not repent, they would become the Lamanites' slaves.

**4   King Noah:** King Noah heard about what Abinadi had said and became angry. He sent his men to bring Abinadi to the palace so he could kill him.

**5   Abinadi with Disguise:** After two years in hiding, Abinadi came back in disguise. *(Have performer put disguise over Abinadi.)* Abinadi began to prophesy again to the people. But he was discovered by the king's men and taken to the king.

**6   Priests:**  Abinadi could not be tricked by the priests' questions. He was not afraid. He knew that God would help him. The priests were amazed at Abinadi's answers.

**7   King Noah & Abinadi (with flashlight):** King Noah was angry and ordered his priests to kill Abinadi. The Holy Ghost protected Abinadi so he could finish saying what the Lord wanted him to say. Abinadi's face was shining. *(Shine flashlight on Abinadi.)* The priests were afraid to touch him.

**8   Jesus:** With God's power, Abinadi told the people about their wickedness. He reminded them of God's commandments. He told them about Jesus Christ and said they must repent and believe in Jesus or they would not be saved.

**9   Alma:** Alma was the only one of the priests who believed Abinadi. He asked King Noah to let Abinadi go. The king was angry with Alma and had him thrown out. Then he told his servants to kill Alma. Alma ran and hid and the servants never found him.

**10   Abinadi and King Noah:** After three days in prison, Abinadi was brought before King Noah. King Noah asked Abinadi to take back all that he had said against the king and his people. King Noah told Abinadi if he did not deny all that he had said, he would be killed.

**11   Abinadi and Fire:** Abinadi knew he had spoken the truth and was willing to die rather than take back what God had sent him to say. King Noah ordered his priests to kill Abinadi. They tied him up, whipped him, and burned him to death. *(Place fire in front of Abinadi.)* Before he died, Abinadi said King Noah would also die by fire.

**12   King Noah:** Soon the Lamanite army came against King Noah and tried to kill him. The king and his followers ran, but the Lamanites caught up with them and began killing them. The king told his men to leave their families and keep running with him.

**13   Priests:** Most of the men who had run away with King Noah were sorry. They wanted to return to their wives, children, and people.

**14   King Noah:** The king ordered the men to stay with him, but the men were so angry with King Noah that they burned him to death, as Abinadi had prophesied. *(Place fire in front of King Noah.)* Then they went back to their families.

my Testimony of Jesus Christ

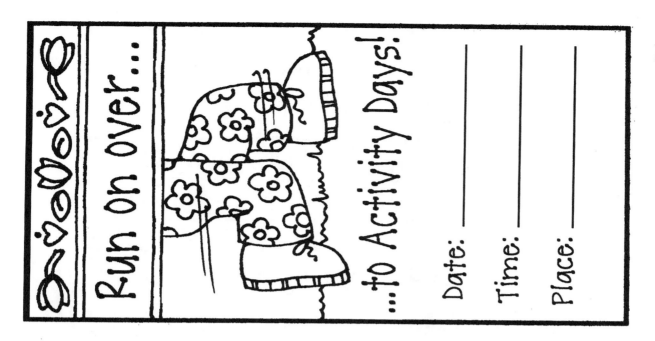

Run on over... ...to Activity Days!

Date:

Time:

Place:

## Learning & Living the Gospel  Goal 7    Word of Wisdom: I Will Blossom and Grow

**ACTIVITY 1:** *Read D&C 89. Discuss how Heavenly Father blesses us when we faithfully live the Word of Wisdom.*

### Word of Wisdom Blossom Blessings (Healthy Flower Pot)

1. Obtain, color, and cut out the *Word of Wisdom Blossom Blessings Healthy Flower Pot* decorations (right). You'll need a healthy plant or flower in a pot.
2. Glue the four *Word of Wisdom Blossom Blessing* cards on wooden craft sticks and place them in the soil of a plant or flowerpot.
3. Review the blessings that come from keeping the Word of Wisdom found on the flowers.
4. Water and care for this plant thinking about the Word of Wisdom each day. Imagine how the plant would wilt and die if it were not fed properly or if you watered it with alcohol or caffeinated drinks.
5. As you give it sunshine and water and watch it grow, nurture your own body and keep the Word of Wisdom by getting the proper nutrition, sleep, exercise, and water and avoid harmful substances.

**ACTIVITY 2:** *Help plan and conduct an activity to teach the Word of Wisdom to others.*

### Bloomin' Good Blessings (Word of Wisdom Block)

1. Obtain, color, and cut out the *Bloomin' Good Blessings* block (shown left).
2. Fold block, fill with cotton balls, and glue tabs to close it.

***Teaching Activity:*** (1) Read D&C 89:18-21. (2) Talk about what is on the block. (3)Take turns rolling the block. If it lands on Bloomin' Good Blessings, tell about someone who is strong who keeps the Word of Wisdom. When it lands on the blessings, talk about that blessing and what it means.

***To Play Game:*** (1) Divide into teams and have each team choose two blessings found on the block that are not the same as the other team's. (2) Roll the block five times. Every time one of your team's blessings, "Bloomin' Good Blessings" or "Keep the Word of Wisdom," come up, you receive a point. When you roll "Keep the Word of Wisdom," tell what you can do to keep the Word of Wisdom, e.g., don't drink or smoke or do drugs, eat meat sparingly, exercise, get enough sleep." (4) Play for 15 minutes and add up points to determine the winning team. (5) Share a healthy treat, giving two treats each to the winning team.

**Word of Wisdom Blessings**

Shall run and not be weary, and shall walk and not faint.

**Word of Wisdom Blessings**

Shall find wisdom and great treasures of knowledge, even hidden treasures.

**Word of Wisdom Blessings**

Shall receive health in their navel and marrow to their bones.

**Word of Wisdom Blessings**

The destroying angel shall pass by them.

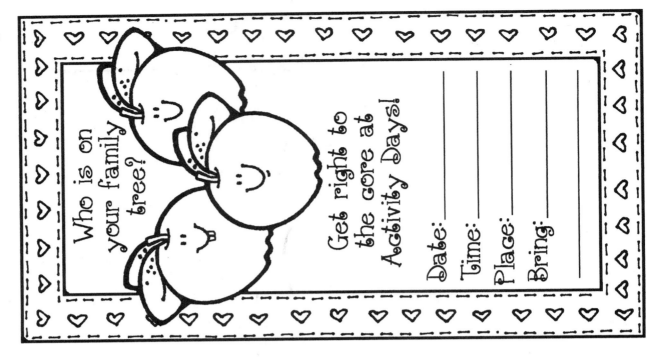

## Learning & Living the Gospel   Goal 8

### Temple Work: My Family Is Blessed

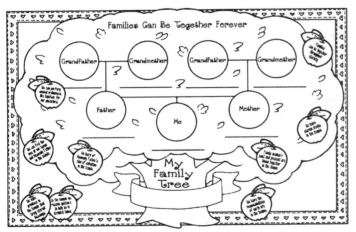

**ACTIVITY 1:** *Prepare a pedigree chart with your name and your parents' and grandparents' names. Prepare a family group record for your family.*

#### Families Can Be Together (Family Tree Pedigree Chart)

1. Obtain and color the *Families Can Be Together Forever: Family Tree Pedigree Chart* (shown left). Cut on the line where indicated on page A and glue to part B.
2. Write the family name on the ribbon.
3. Copy and cut out pictures and glue them in the circles above the matching names on the chart.

**ACTIVITY 2:** *Share a family story.*

#### Family History (Appealing Family Story Sketch)

1. Obtain and color the *Story Sketch* (shown left).
2. Write or mount a written family story on the page you wish to share.

**ACTIVITY 3:** *Discuss how performing temple work blesses families.*

#### Fruits of the Temple (Family Tree Decorations)

1. Obtain, color, and cut out the *Fruits of the Temple Family Tree Decorations* (shown above on the *Family Tree Pedigree Chart*).
2. Post the fruit on your family tree, showing how performing temple work blesses families.
3. Talk about each as you place them on the tree.

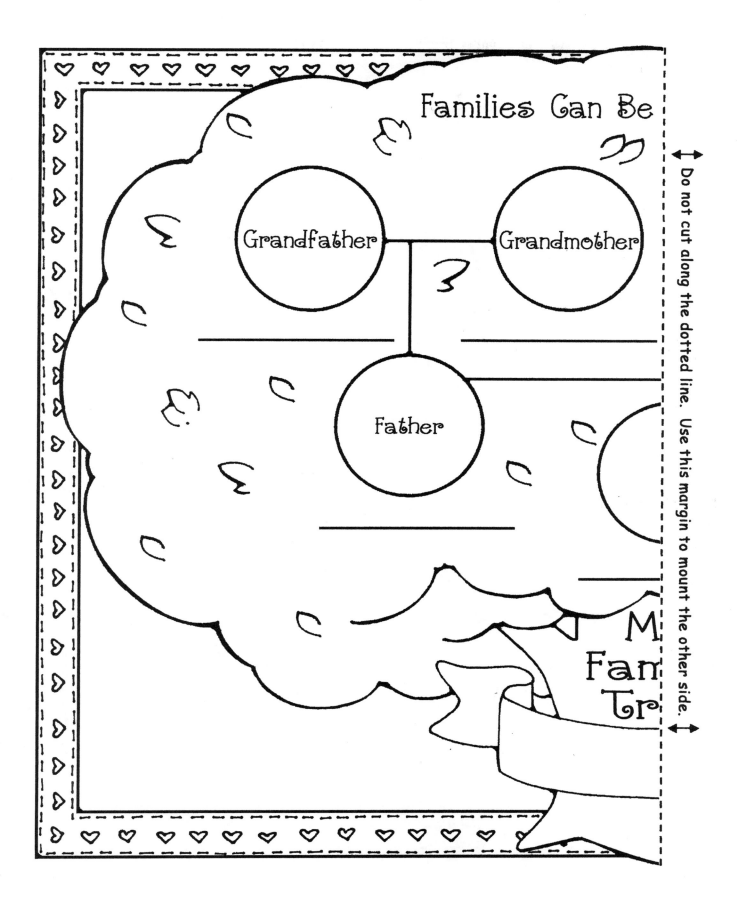

Families Can Be

Grandfather ——— Grandmother

Father

M
Fam
Tr

Together Forever

Grandfather

Grandmother

Mother

Me

Cut carefully along the inside of the dotted line.

# Appealing Family Story Sketch

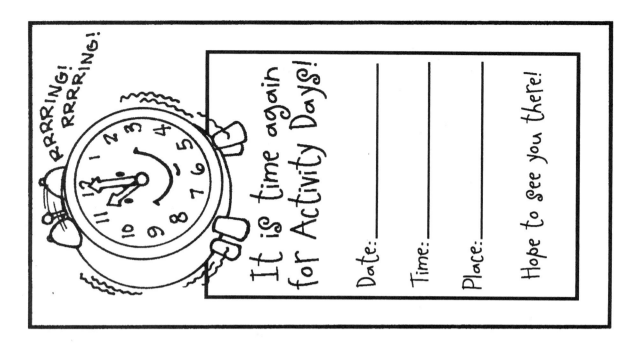

It is time again for Activity Days!

RRRRING! RRRRING!

Date: _____

Time: _____

Place: _____

Hope to see you there!

## Learning & Living the Gospel  Goal 9    Choose the Right: I Will Make Good Choices

**ACTIVITY 1:** *Learn to sing "Choose the Right" (Hymns, no. 239).*

**ACTIVITY 2:** *Explain what agency is and what it means to be responsible for your choices. Discuss how making good choices has helped you develop greater faith.*

### Choosing a Consequence (Spin-the-Bottle)

Obtain, color, and cut out the *Choosing a Consequence Spin-the-Bottle Game* label, wordstrips, and signs (shown right).
**To Make:** Glue the label and game rules on a bottle with a lid. Fill the bottle with the "smile" and "frown" wordstrips. Close the lid. See details on label to set up and play the game using the "Immediate Consequence," "Future Consequence," and "Eternal Consequence." signs.

### Choosing a Consequence Spin-the-Bottle Game

**To Set Up Game:** Tape to the floor or table in the center of a circle the "Immediate Consequence," "Future Consequence," and "Eternal Consequence" signs.
**To Play:** Have players sit around in a circle. Teams take turns having a player spin the bottle in the center inside the signs. The bottle neck should point to one of the signs. If neck is on the border of the signs, choose the sign to the right of the bottle neck. Player pulls out a "smile" or "frown" wordstrip and reads it aloud. Player names the consequence for that action that matches the type of consequence for where the bottle neck is pointing. Example: the "Immediate Consequence" for "Stay up late" is you are tired the next day. Collect the smiles. When the bottle is empty, the team with the most "smiles" wins.

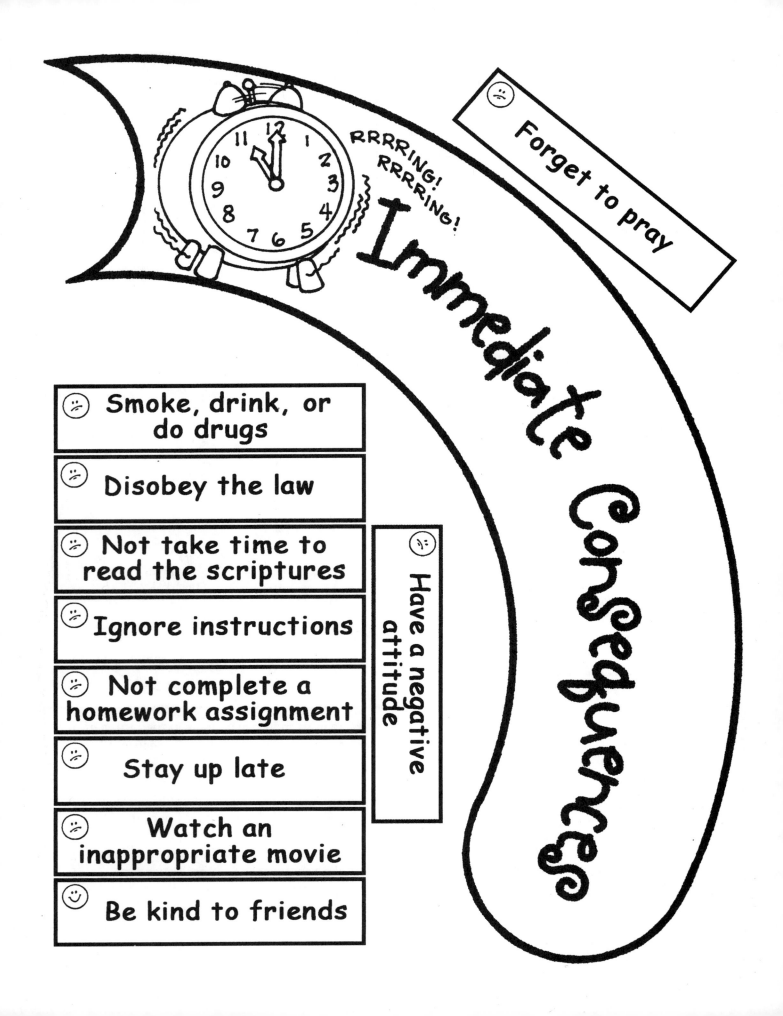

Immediate Consequences

Forget to pray

Smoke, drink, or do drugs

Disobey the law

Not take time to read the scriptures

Ignore instructions

Not complete a homework assignment

Stay up late

Watch an inappropriate movie

Be kind to friends

Have a negative attitude

RRRRING! RRRRING!

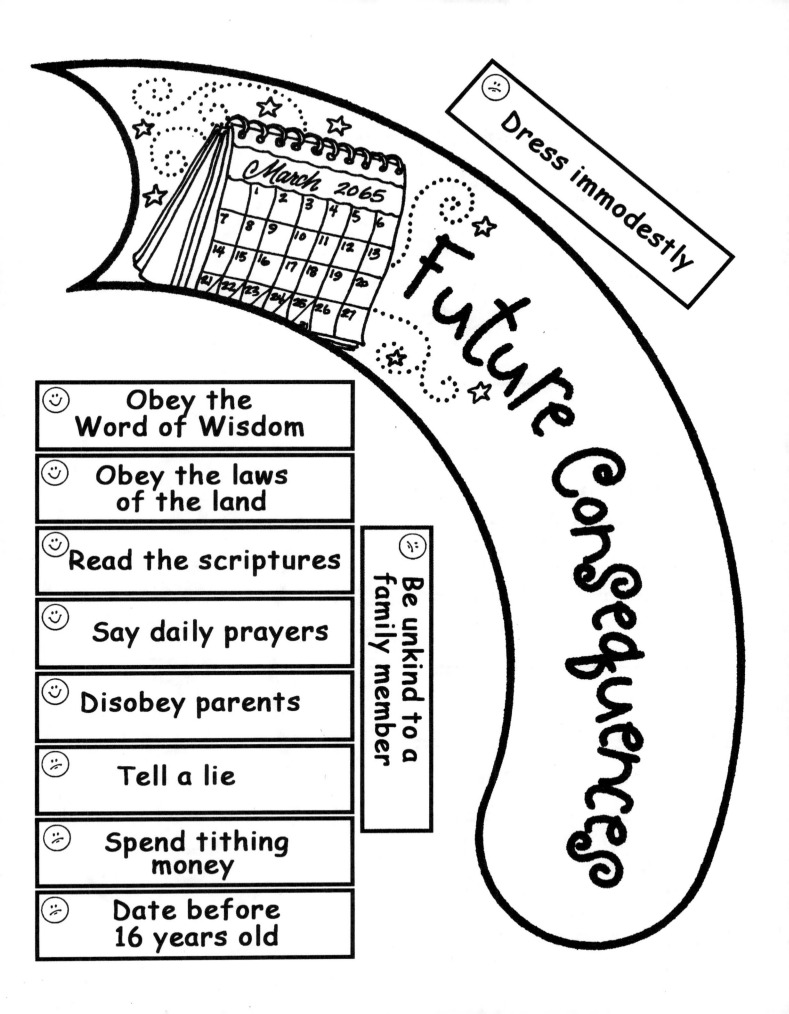

Future Consequences

March 2065

Dress immodestly

Obey the Word of Wisdom

Obey the laws of the land

Read the scriptures

Say daily prayers

Disobey parents

Tell a lie

Spend tithing money

Date before 16 years old

Be unkind to a family member

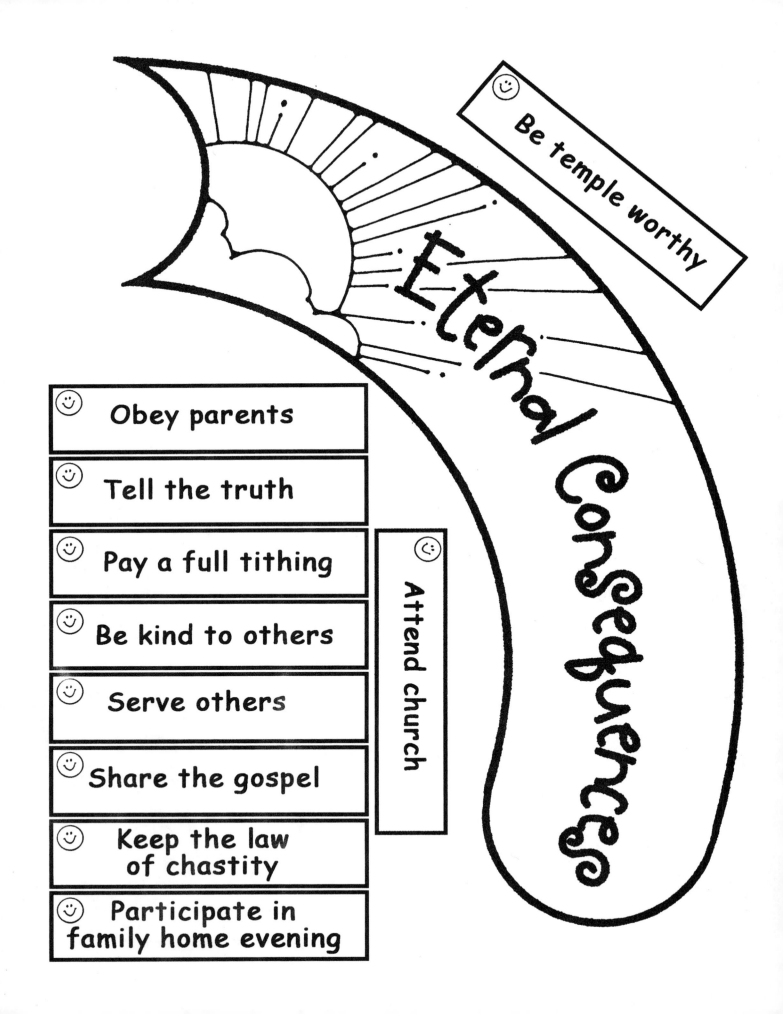

Be temple worthy

Eternal Consequences

Obey parents

Tell the truth

Pay a full tithing

Be kind to others

Serve others

Share the gospel

Keep the law of chastity

Participate in family home evening

Attend church

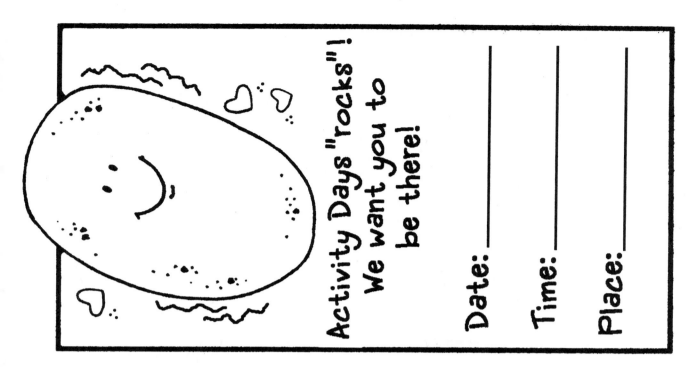

Activity Days "rocks"! We want you to be there!

Date: _____

Time: _____

Place: _____

Learning & Living the Gospel  Goal 10          Gospel Living: I Will Build a Strong Testimony

**ACTIVITY:** *Plan and complete your own activity that will help you learn and live the gospel (write the activity in your "Faith in God" booklet, p.7).*

## Wise Man "Built His House Upon a Rock" (Testimony Building Project)

Instead of building your house upon sand to be washed away, build your house upon rock like the wise man. Your house will not fall if you build it upon the gospel of Jesus Christ. Jesus is the rock, our sure foundation. By building our house upon the rock we will be able to withstand "winds of the devil" and destruction. Read 3 Nephi 11:40, Matthew 7:24-27, and Helaman 5:12.

1. Obtain, color, and cut out the house and rock pieces (shown right).

2. Build your house upon the rock by increasing your testimony.

*Step 1: Build Your Foundation:* Post the rocks on a door or wall. Then write on each rock a gospel principle you will obey and make a specific goal for each (see ideas below).

*Step 2: Strengthen Your Foundation:* Learn about and live each of the gospel principles you have chosen.

*Step 3: Build Upon the Rock:* For each gospel principle you have lived, add to the visual, building your sure foundation.

*Gospel Principles and Testimony Builders:*  FAITH, FASTING, FORGIVENESS, HONORING PARENTS, HONESTY, MISSIONARY WORK, MODEST DRESS, OBEDIENCE, REPENTANCE, REVELATION, REVERENCE, HONORING SABBATH, SACRAMENT, SCRIPTURES, SERVICE, TITHING, WORD OF WISDOM, OBEDIENCE, PRAYER

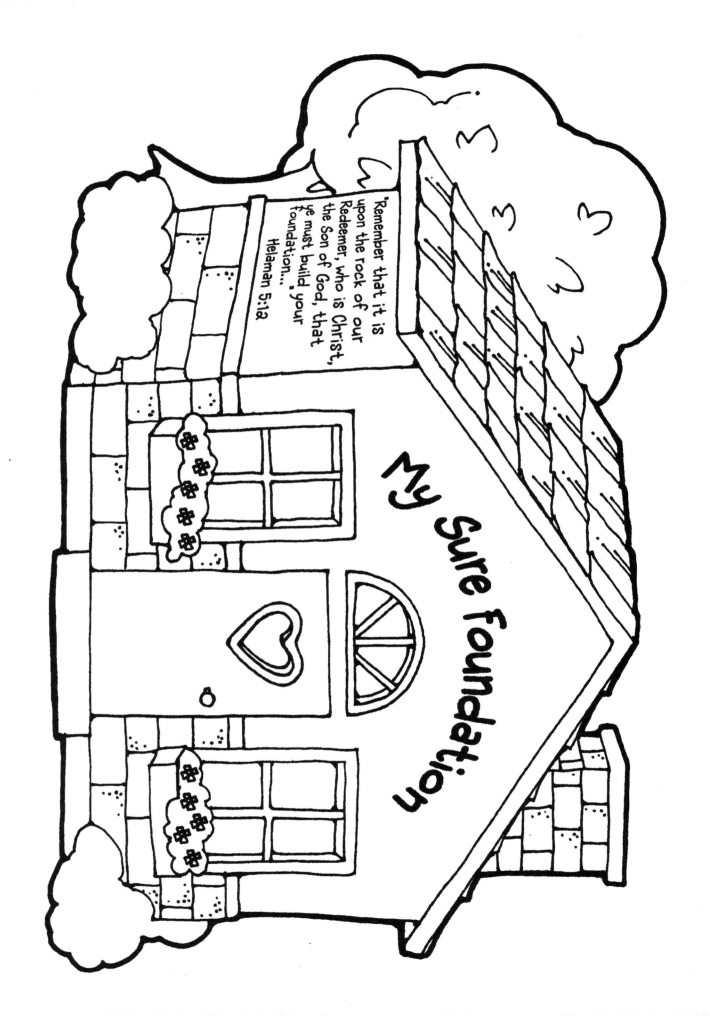

"Remember that it is upon the rock of our Redeemer, who is Christ, the Son of God, that ye must build your foundation..."

Helaman 5:1a

My Sure Foundation

Sure Foundation Principle

I will: _____

_____

_____

Sure Foundation Principle

I will: _____

_____

_____

Sure Foundation Principle

I will: _____

_____

_____

Sure Foundation Principle

I will: _____

_____

_____

Sure Foundation Principle

I will: _____

_____

_____

Sure Foundation Principle

I will: _____

_____

_____

Sure Foundation Principle

I will: _____

_____

_____

Sure Foundation Principle

I will: _____

_____

_____

## 1. COVENANTS: I Will Remain Faithful

<u>(Promise Pudding)</u>. Give each girl a small container of pudding.

*Thought:* Talk about the promises we make at baptism to keep Heavenly Father's commandments. With every bite, have girls name these commandments. Tell them that just as pudding is smooth, we too can become smooth (perfect) as we strive to live the teachings of the gospel of Jesus Christ.

## 2. PRAYER: I Will Pray Sincerely

<u>(Prayer Memory Mints)</u>. Give each girl a bag of mints with this reminder note:

> Heavenly Father "mint" for us to pray to Him each day so that He can guide and comfort us. He will answer our prayers if we pray sincerely.

## 3. HOLY GHOST: The Holy Ghost Will Help Me Throughout My Life

<u>("Free Your Mind of Clutter" Cookies)</u>. For each girl, frost a sugar cookie and top with "clutter" (dried fruit, chocolate chips, candies, broken lifesavers). Next, frost a sugar cookie for each girl and decorate it with a simple frosting smiling face.

*Thought:* As girls eat, remind them to keep their lives free from clutter (noisy music, too much television, and things that are not of value). This way we can make room in our minds and hearts so that the Holy Ghost can guide us. We can find happiness as we make life decisions that are eternal.

## 4. OBEDIENCE: I Will Follow the Prophet

<u>(Butterfinger Candy Bars)</u>. Give each girl a small Butterfinger candy bar. Open the bars and look inside. The candy inside looks like tree bark.

*Thought:* Tell girls, "Each year a tree grows strong as it reaches toward the sun, receiving moisture to grow. We too grow each year as we listen to the prophet. Our spirits and testimonies can grow strong from learning the gospel and obeying the commandments.

## 5. PRAYER: I Will Stay Close to Heavenly Father

<u>(Search and Ponder Pretzels or Bread Sticks)</u>. Give each girl some straight pretzels or bread sticks, or have them bake their own straight bread sticks.

*Thought:* As they eat, read Matthew 22:29, Alma 7:9; 37:44, 1 Nephi 8; 12:17; 15:12-25, and D&C 88:63. Tell girls that the pretzels or bread sticks remind us of the straight and narrow path that leads us back to our Heavenly Father. We can stay on the path if we hold onto the iron rod, the word of God found in the scriptures and through prayer. As we search, ponder, and pray about the scriptures each day, we can keep the heavenly communication lines open and be guided throughout our lives. Happiness can come each day if we strive to stay on the straight and narrow path.

## 6. TESTIMONY: I Know Jesus Christ Lives

(Testimony Hourglass Cereal Bars). Make an hourglass-shaped marshmallow-and-cereal treat (below) and use it as follows.

*To Make Treat:* Melt 3 tablespoons margarine and marshmallows in a large bowl. Add one of the following marshmallow choices: (1) 10 ounce package of marshmallows, (2) 40 regular sized marshmallows, or (3) 4 cups of miniature marshmallows. Add 6 cups of rice puff cereal and stir. Lightly butter a 12x9x2-inch pan and press marshmallow treat in pan. Cut treats into 6" x 2" bars and wrap in clear plastic wrap. Tie two different strings tightly in a bow in the middle of the treat to create an hourglass shape.

*Thought:* Tell girls that the hourglass represents our time here on earth, and this hourglass-shaped treat reminds us of the sweet blessings Heavenly Father has given us. He has given us a special gift with no strings attached (cut off one string). This gift is the gift of resurrection. Everyone will live again with a resurrected body. The second gift of eternal life has a string attached (leave second string on). We must earn this special gift if we want to spend all of eternity with our families and with our Heavenly Father and Jesus who love us. Remember our potential is great and we can receive this gift if we use our time wisely.

## 7. WORD OF WISDOM: I Will Blossom and Grow

(Healthy Snacks). Have girls bring their favorite healthy snack to share. Or provide healthy snacks, e.g., slice of whole-grain bread with peanut butter or butter and honey, fruit, vegetables, granola bars. *Option:* Vegetables, e.g., radishes, carrots, celery can be cut into flower and leaf shapes to remind girls to blossom and grow.

## 8. TEMPLE WORK: My Family Is Blessed

(Eternity Ring Doughnuts). Serve girls cake doughnuts that represent eternal marriage, having no end, lasting forever and ever if both husband and wife obey Heavenly Father's commandments and keep his and her own covenants. Children can also be sealed to their parents forever if they too obey. Temple work helps seal families together forever.

## 9. CHOOSE THE RIGHT: I Will Make Good Choices

(Thumbs-Up Thumbprint Cookies). Press your thumb into a ball of sugar-cookie dough and bake. Tell girls that thumbs-up means "good going." Let's try each day to make thumbs-up choices.

## 10. GOSPEL LIVING: I Will Build a Strong Testimony

(TESTIMONY Treats). Any food that begins with the letter in the word TESTIMONY, e.g., taffy, egg, sandwich, toast, iceberg lettuce, mustard, orange, nut or noodle, yogurt or yam.

*Activity 1:* Place food items on a tray for girls to see, then play the memory game. Girls can look at the tray for 60 seconds (identify each item for them). Remove tray, then give each girl a pencil and paper to write what they saw on the tray. Try to write the word "TESTIMONY." Award a treat to everyone, but a double treat to those who spelled the word. *Treat Ideas:* dyed, hard-boiled egg, orange, nuts.

*Activity 2:* If you don't have much time, simply have girls write "TESTIMONY" by placing treats in order, e.g., toast first and egg second.

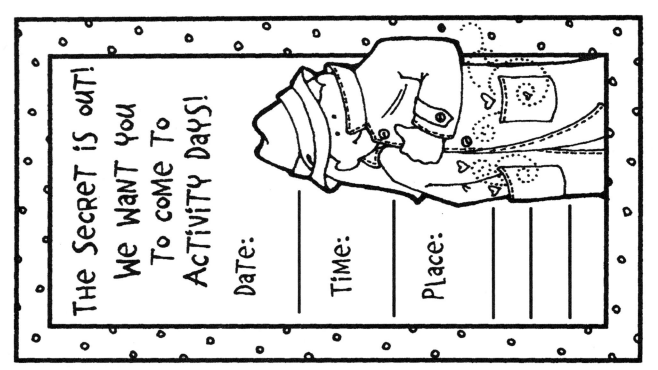

The Secret is out!
We want you
To come to
Activity Days!

DaTe: _____

Time: _____

Place: _____

Serving Others  Goal 1        Samaritan Service: Service Helps My Faith Grow Stronger

**ACTIVITY 1:** *Read and discuss the parable of the good Samaritan (see Luke 10:30–37).*

Discussion:

Talk about how the good Samaritan gave of his time, talent, and means to help someone in need.

**ACTIVITY 2:** *Plan and complete a service project that helps a family member or neighbor.*

Good Samaritan (Secret Service Project)

1. Obtain and color the *Good Samaritan Secret Service Project* planner (shown right).
2. To plan your service project, answer the questions on the planner, e.g., "who," "what," etc. to plan your service project.
3. Assign certain girls certain tasks on the planner. Then complete service project in secret(showing anonymous service) if possible.

**ACTIVITY 3:** *After completing the project, discuss how it helped your faith grow stronger and record it on the planner.*

Good Samaritan Secret Service Project

<u>Who</u> We Want To Serve:_____

<u>What</u> We Want To Do:_____
_____
_____

<u>Where</u> We Will Go:_____

<u>When</u> We Will Serve:_____

<u>Why</u> We Want To Serve:_____

My Assignment:_____
_____

Complete after project:
How did this project help my faith grow stronger?
_____
_____
_____
_____

# Good Samaritan Secret Service Project

WHO WE WANT TO SERVE: _____

_____

WHAT WE WANT TO DO: _____

_____

_____

_____

WHERE WE WILL GO: _____

WHEN WE WILL SERVE: _____

WHY WE WANT TO SERVE: _____

_____

MY ASSIGNMENT: _____

_____

_____

COMPLETE AFTER PROJECT:
HOW DID THIS PROJECT HELP MY
FAITH GROW STRONGER?

_____

_____

_____

_____

Buzz on over
to Activity Days!

Date: _____

Time: _____

Place: _____

You must "bee" there!

## Serving Others   Goal 2

## Gratitude: I Will Express Appreciation

**ACTIVITY:** *Write a letter to a teacher, your parents, or your grandparents telling them what you appreciate and respect about them.*

### A "Buzz"illion Thanks! Jot-a-Thought (Stationery and Envelope)

1. Obtain, color, and cut out the *"Buzz"illion Thanks! Jot-a-Thought Stationery and Envelope* (shown left) for each person for whom you want to send a letter and express appreciation.

2. Use the *Jot-a-Thought Letter Starter* ideas below or make up your own to write a letter on the stationery as detailed above.

### Jot-a-Thought Letter Starters:

| | |
|---|---|
| I want to be like you because . . . | You're so cool to teach me the rules of . . . |
| You made me feel special because . . . | I'm glad you're a friend because . . . |
| I admire you because . . . | I hope it's not too late to tell you how much I appreciate . . . |
| I love you because . . . | Knowing you has been great because . . . |
| You make me want to be better because . . . | It's nice to know I have a friend like you because . . . |
| I appreciate you when you . . . | When I think of our friendship I think of . . . |
| I'm thankful for you because . . . | Good friends are hard to find. Thanks for . . . |
| The top 10 things I like about you are . . . | Thanks for your patience and your love in . . . |
| It's nice to know that you care about . . . | It's really a treat be in your class because . . . |

Cut off outside margin so letter will fit into envelope.

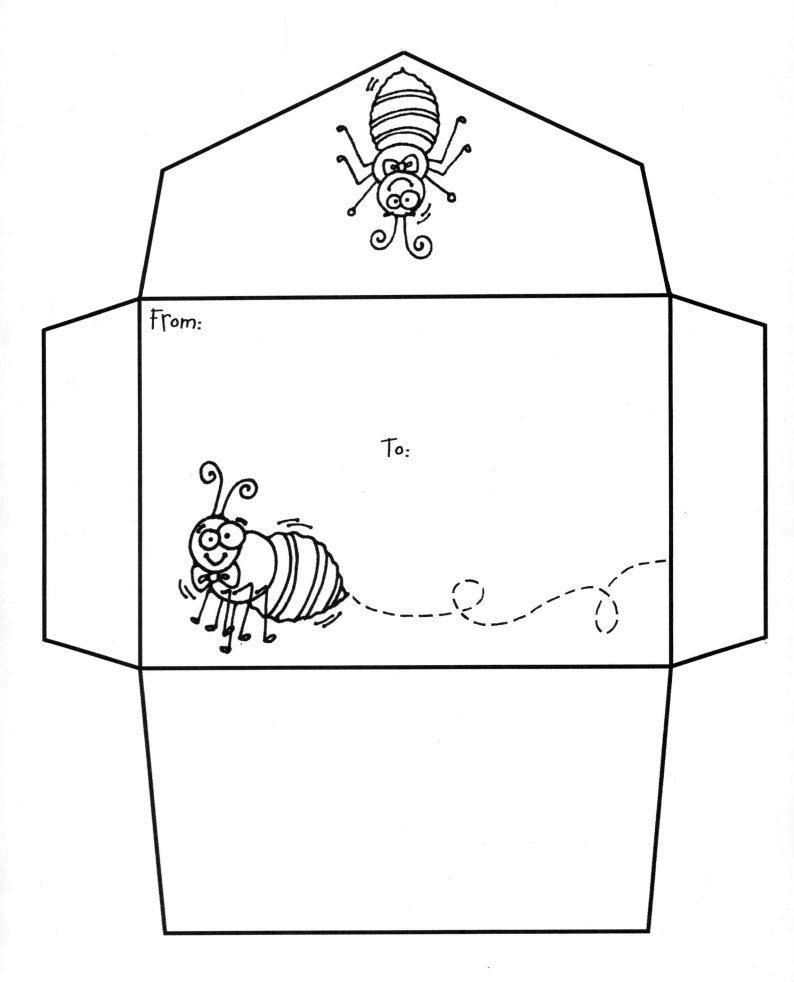

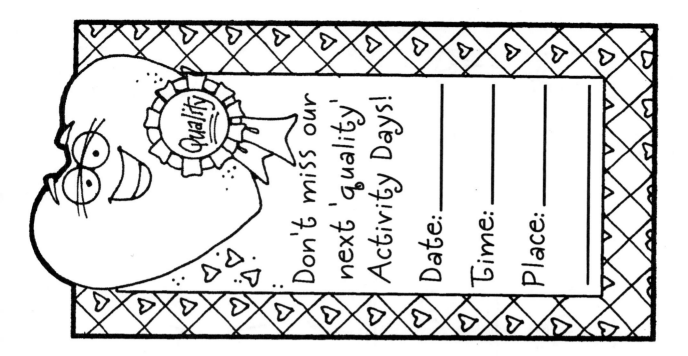

Don't miss our
next 'quality'
Activity Days!

Date:

Time:

Place:

Serving Others  Goal 3          Character: I Will Develop Sweet-Spirit Qualities

**ACTIVITY 1:** *Make a list of the qualities you like in a person. Choose one quality to develop in yourself.*

Sweet-Spirit (Quality Quiz Match Game,
Quality Quiz, and "I Am" Quality Mirror Motivator)

Obtain, color, and cut out two sets of the *Quality Quiz Match Game Cards,* one *Sweet-Spirit Quality Quiz,* and one "I Am" Mirror Motivator (shown right). *Optional:* Reward with sweet and sour candies.

• *Quality Quiz Match Game:* Divide into teams and play a match game with the *Quality Quiz Match Game Cards.* The team with the most matches wins. This will help you think up positive qualities.

• *Quality Quiz:* Compete for five minutes having each girl think up the most sweet- spirit qualities she can and writing them on her *Sweet-Spirit Quality Quiz.* Take turns reading aloud these qualities you like in people. Check those read against your own list. If yours have been listed by another, check them. List those that are not on your list on the back of your *Quiz* for inspiration. The winner is the one who has the most unique qualities on their list that were not listed by others.

• *"I Am" Quality Mirror Motivator:* Choose a quality from the *Sweet-Spirit Quality Quiz* card that you would like to develop, then write it here. Below, write what you will do to develop this quality. Draw in your own hairstyle around the face. Post it on the mirror to remind you of this sweet-spirit quality you wish to develop.

**ACTIVITY 2:** *Discuss how showing respect and kindness strengthens you, your family, and others (write these below).*

Respect:

Kindness:

I Am: _____

I will develop
this quality by:

_____
_____
_____
_____

Sweet-Spirit
Quality Quiz

List as many sweet-
spirit qualities that
you like in a person
as you can.

Quality

## Serving Others Goal 4        Thoughtful Chef: I Will Create Nutritious Meals

**ACTIVITY:** *Plan, prepare, and serve a nutritious meal.*

### Thoughtful Chef (Skill-Meal Recipes)

1. Obtain, color, and cut out the *Thoughtful Chef Skill-Meal Recipes* (shown right).

2. Plan, prepare, and share several recipes to develop some of the following skills. In the recipes enclosed you will be able to develop some of the skills listed below. While trying these recipes, identify and underline the skills and tools that you used below.

*Cooking Skills:*
- bake (biscuits, bread, cake, or cookies)
- brown (meat) · cook (eggs or noodles)
- core (lettuce, apples, pears)
- cut out (biscuits, bread, or cookie dough)
- drain (cooked macaroni, canned food)
- egg (separate, mix, whip egg whites)
- fry (vegetables, meat) · grating (cheese)
- grease (pan) · knead (dough)
- measuring (wet and dry ingredients)
- melt (chocolate) · mash (potatoes)
- mix (batter) · shred (cabbage or lettuce)
- pair, peel, and cut up (vegetables)
- roll out (cookie dough or pastry)
- simmer (soup) · snip (parsley & herbs)
- stir (muffins or batter) · whip (cream)
- thicken (gravy or sauce)

*Cooking Tools:*
- knives (use of)
- measuring cups & spoons
- thermometers
- can openers
- bottle openers
- pastry brush
- rolling pin
- kitchen sheers
- cheese slicer
- pizza cutter
- citrus zester
- pastry bag
- pastry blender · colander · cutting board · chopper · funnel
- grater · mixing bowls · pans · pepper grinder · mixer · skewers
- spatulas · spoons · pancake turners · parchment paper
- potato masher · wire whisk · blender · food processor

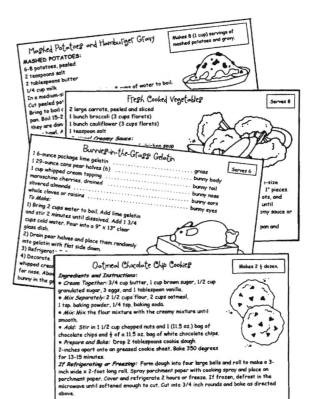

**Mashed Potatoes and Hamburger Gravy**     Makes 8 (1 cup) servings of mashed potatoes and gravy.

**MASHED POTATOES:**
6-8 potatoes, peeled
2 teaspoons salt
2 tablespoons butter
1/4 cup milk
In a medium-si
Cut peeled pot
Bring to boil (
pan. Boil 15-2
they are don
howl. A

**Fresh Cooked Vegetables**     Serves 8
2 large carrots, peeled and sliced
1 bunch broccoli (3 cups florets)
1 bunch cauliflower (3 cups florets)
1 teaspoon salt
chicken soup

**Bunnies-in-the-Grass Gelatin**     Serves 6
1 6-ounce package lime gelatin
1 29-ounce cans pear halves (6)
1 cup whipped cream topping . . . . . . . . . . . grass
maraschino cherries, drained . . . . . . . . . . bunny body
slivered almonds . . . . . . . . . . . . . . . . . . . bunny tail
whole cloves or raisins . . . . . . . . . . . . . . . bunny nose
To Make: . . . . . . . . . . . . . . . . . . . . . . . . bunny ears
1) Bring 2 cups water to boil. Add lime gelatin . . bunny eyes
and stir 2 minutes until dissolved. Add 1 3/4
cups cold water. Pour into a 9" x 13" clear
glass dish.
2) Drain pear halves and place them randomly
into gelatin with flat side down.
3) Refrigerat-
4) Decorate
whipped crea
for nose. Abo
bunny in the g

**Oatmeal Chocolate Chip Cookies**     Makes 2 ½ dozen.

*Ingredients and Instructions:*
- *Cream Together:* 3/4 cup butter, 1 cup brown sugar, 1/2 cup granulated sugar, 3 eggs, and 1 tablespoon vanilla.
- *Mix Separately:* 2 1/2 cups flour, 2 cups oatmeal, 1 tsp. baking powder, 1/4 tsp. baking soda.
- *Mix:* Mix the flour mixture with the creamy mixture until smooth.
- *Add:* Stir in 1 1/2 cup chopped nuts and 1 (11.5 oz.) bag of chocolate chips and ½ of a 11.5 oz. bag of white chocolate chips.
- *Prepare and Bake:* Drop 2 tablespoons cookie dough 2-inches apart onto a greased cookie sheet. Bake 350 degrees for 13-15 minutes.
- *If Refrigerating or Freezing:* Form dough into four large balls and roll to make a 3-inch wide x 2-foot long roll. Spray parchment paper with cooking spray and place on parchment paper. Cover and refrigerate 2 hours or freeze. If frozen, defrost in the microwave until softened enough to cut. Cut into 3/4 inch rounds and bake as directed above.

## Mashed Potatoes and Hamburger Gravy

Makes 8 (1 cup) servings of mashed potatoes and gravy.

### MASHED POTATOES:

6-8 potatoes, peeled
2 teaspoons salt
2 tablespoons butter
1/4 cup milk

In a medium-sized saucepan, bring 8 cups of water to boil. Cut peeled potatoes in half and add to water. Add salt. Bring to boil and reduce heat to medium, placing lid on pan. Boil 15-20 minutes. If a fork pierces through easily, they are done. Drain in a colander, reserving water to use in gravy.* Place potatoes in a large bowl. Add butter and milk, then mash them, adding more milk or butter if needed. Top with 1 tablespoon butter. Cover with foil to keep warm.

### HAMBURGER GRAVY:

1 lb hamburger
1/4 teaspoon pepper
1 (1.2 oz.) package
brown gravy mix
*2 cups water

In a large skillet, brown hamburger, adding ½ of a chopped onion (optional), salt, and pepper. Keep chopping and stirring until browned on medium-high heat for 5-10 minutes. Stir flour into meat and add potato water and stir, simmering.

---

## Fresh Cooked Vegetables

Serves 8

2 large carrots, peeled and sliced
1 bunch broccoli (3 cups florets)
1 bunch cauliflower (3 cups florets)
1 teaspoon salt

*Optional Creamy Sauce:*
1 10 3/4-ounce can cream of chicken soup
3 ounces (4 slices) Swiss cheese, torn
1/2 teaspoon dried basil
2 tablespoon butter

**To Make Vegetables:** Cut stems off broccoli leaving 2-inches of each stock. Pull cauliflower apart and cut into bite-size pieces. Using a carrot/potato peeler, remove peeling from carrot and cut into 1" pieces. Bring 2 cups water to boil in a large saucepan. Add broccoli, cauliflower, carrots, and salt. Bring to boil, reduce to medium heat and add lid. Cook 10-12 minutes or until tender. Strain vegetables in a colander. Place in a bowl and gently stir in creamy sauce or 2 tablespoons melted butter.

**To Make Sauce:** Add cream of chicken soup, cheese, basil, and butter to a pan and warm, then stir together.

## Bunnies-in-the-Grass Gelatin

**Serves 6**

1 6-ounce package lime gelatin . . . . . . . . . . . . . . . . . . . . . . . grass
1 29-ounce cans pear halves (6) . . . . . . . . . . . . . . . . . bunny body
1 cup whipped cream topping . . . . . . . . . . . . . . . . . . . . bunny tail
maraschino cherries, drained . . . . . . . . . . . . . . . . . . bunny nose
slivered almonds . . . . . . . . . . . . . . . . . . . . . . . . . . . . . bunny ears
whole cloves or raisins . . . . . . . . . . . . . . . . . . . . . . . . bunny eyes

*To Make:*

1) Bring 2 cups water to boil. Add lime gelatin
and stir 2 minutes until dissolved. Add 1 3/4
cups cold water. Pour into a 9" x 13" clear glass
dish.
2) Refrigerate 2-3 hours until gelatin is firm.
3) Drain pear halves and place them randomly
onto gelatin with flat side down.
4) Decorate. Place a heaping tablespoon
whipped cream at the fat end for bunny's tail. Place a whole cherry at the narrow end
for nose. Above nose place almond ears and clove or raisin eyes.
5) Give each person a bunny in the grass.

## Oatmeal Chocolate Chip Cookies

**Makes 2 ½ dozen.**

**Ingredients and Instructions:**

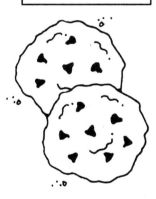

• *Cream Together:* 3/4 cup butter, 1 cup brown sugar, 1/2 cup
granulated sugar, 3 eggs, and 1 tablespoon vanilla.
• *Mix Separately:* 2 1/2 cups flour, 2 cups oatmeal,
1 tsp. baking powder, 1/4 tsp. baking soda.
• *Mix:* Mix the flour mixture with the creamy mixture until
smooth.
• *Add:* Stir in 1 1/2 cup chopped nuts and 1 (11.5 oz.) bag of
chocolate chips and ½ of a 11.5 oz. bag of white chocolate chips.
• *Prepare and Bake:* Drop 2 tablespoons cookie dough
2-inches apart onto a greased cookie sheet. Bake 350 degrees
for 13-15 minutes.

**If Refrigerating or Freezing:** Form dough into four large balls and roll to make a 3-
inch wide x 2-foot long roll. Spray parchment paper with cooking spray and place on
parchment paper. Cover and refrigerate 2 hours or freeze. If frozen, defrost in the
microwave until softened enough to cut. Cut into 3/4-inch rounds and bake as directed
above.

We "wooly" want you there!

Come to Activity Days!

Date: _____

Time: _____

Place: _____

## Serving Others    Goal 5

## Child Care: Learn Babysitting Basics

**ACTIVITY 1:** *Entertain children with songs or games you have learned or made yourself.*

### Old McDonald Song and Game (Music and Visuals)

Obtain, color, and cut out the *Old McDonald Had a Farm* song sheet and the *Old McDonald* song and game visuals (shown left).

• *Old McDonald Song Visuals:* Use them to teach children this song, placing visuals on sticks for children to hold.

• *Old McDonald Game Visuals:* With a safety pin, pin a "farmer" or "animal" visual (shown left) on the back of each child playing, and have them imitate their animal while playing the game.

• *To Set Up Game:* Place a 1-foot paper circle in the center of the room (a safe spot where one child can stand). Form boundary lines outside circle with strings to make a corral so "animals" don't go too far from the circle.

• *To Play Game:* Have "animals" (players) run around the circle to keep away from the "farmer" (another player) who tries to tag them. To be safe, "animals" can stand in the center spot for 3 seconds. When caught, the "animal" becomes the "farmer," and they switch signs and roles.

**ACTIVITY 2:** *Show that you know how to care for and nurture a young child.*

Obtain and color the *Barnyard Babysitting Basics* Poster and *Get Your Ducks-in-a-Row Emergency List* (shown right).

### Barnyard Babysitting Basics (Poster)

Memorize these basics to be a good sitter.

### Get Your Ducks-in-a-Row (Emergency List)

Write important things to remember while interviewing parents before they leave.

# Old MacDonald Had a Farm

Old MacDonald had a farm, E-I-E-I-O,
And on his farm he had a *cow*, E-I-E-I-O,
With a *moo-moo* here and a *moo-moo* there,
Here a *moo*, there a *moo*, everywhere a *moo – moo*.
Old MacDonald had a farm, E-I-E-I-O.

Pig . . . oink–oink
Horse . . . neigh–neigh
Chicken . . . cluck–cluck
Dog . . . bow–wow
Sheep . . . baa–baa

# Get Your Ducks-in-a-Row Babysitter's List

## Family Information

Parent's Names: _____

Home Address: _____

Home Phone: _____

Dad's Work or Cell Phone: _____

Mom's Work or Cell Phone: _____

| Children: | Ages: | Special Needs: |
|-----------|-------|----------------|
| | | |
| | | |
| | | |
| | | |

Parents located at: _____

Parents will return by: _____

Special Instructions: _____

_____

Notes to Parents: _____

_____

_____

_____

## Emergency Information

Fire or Police: Dial 911

Neighbor 1: _____ Phone: _____ Address: _____

Neighbor 2: _____ Phone: _____ Address: _____

# BARNYARD BABYSITTING BASICS:

### You'll Be the Cat's Meow Babysitter If You Try These:

- Don't be a quiet mouse, announce that you are interested in babysitting.
- Buzz on over to a class or library to learn about first aid and babysitting.
- Don't be like a goat and over-"charge." Ask for average babysitter's pay.

### Before Parents Leave:

- Be a lightening bug and bug parents for emergency numbers to find in a flash! Also ask how parents or neighbors can be reached.
- Fly through the house before parents leave and lock windows and doors.

### After Parents Leave:

- Keep your ducks in a row. Keep children with you at all times.
- Protect the children. Don't be sheepish about enforcing the safety rules.
- Feed the little chicks what their parents want them to eat, and don't be a pig. Bring a few of your own snacks.
- Don't get horse by yelling at the children. Be patient, loving, and kind.

### Safety Rules:

- Be sly like a fox when you answer calls. Never say you are the babysitter.
- Hop to it and turn the outside lights on when it gets dark.
- Be a chicken and don't open the door to strangers.
   - Be dog-gone careful and call the police if you sense there is an intruder outside. Never go outside to investigate. Keep blinds closed.

Come find out what really "manners" at Activity Days!

Date: _____

Time: _____

Place: _____

It'll take you in the right direction!

Serving Others  Goal 6        Manners: I Will Practice Good Manners and Courtesy

**ACTIVITY:** *Learn about and practice good manners and courtesy.*

Manners Meter  (Roleplay Rating Game and Practicing Tool)

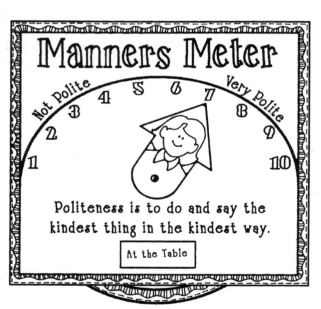

**To Make Game and Tool:** Obtain, color, and cut out the *Manners Meter Game and Practicing Tool* and situation cards (shown left). Cut out the window on the front so situation—e.g., "On the Telephone"—can show through as you turn the wheel. Place the wheel behind and the arrow in the center-front of meter, securing parts with a brad.

**Manners Meter Rating Game:**

1. Tell players, "Manners is a guide to getting along with other people." Review the manners motto in #4 below.

2. Divide players into groups of two or three and assign situation cards, dividing up cards. Give teams 20 minutes to rehearse. For each card they should act out a "good manner" and a "bad manner" to dramatize the situation on the card. Exaggerate these to get a very bad or a very good rating on each as follows.

3. When the actors come out they announce the situation, e.g., "At church." Then the audience turns their wheel to that situation on their meter. Then the actors put on their performance.

4. The audience must judge the manner according to this manners motto:   *"Politeness is to do and say the kindest thing in the kindest way."*  The audience judges the skit when it is over by saying "good manner" or "bad manner," then turns the arrow on their meter from 6-10 if it is a "good manner" or 1-4 if it is a "bad manner."

5. Talk about manners and why they are important.

*Manners Meter Practicing Tool:* Turn the meter each day to indicate where you need to practice better manners. Draw a card for that manner and practice it that day. At the end of the day turn the arrow to indicate how well you did ( 1 is the lowest and 10 is the highest).

# Manners Meter

Not Polite

Very Polite

1 2 3 4 5 6 7 8 9 10

Politeness is to do and say the kindest thing in the kindest way.

Cut Out

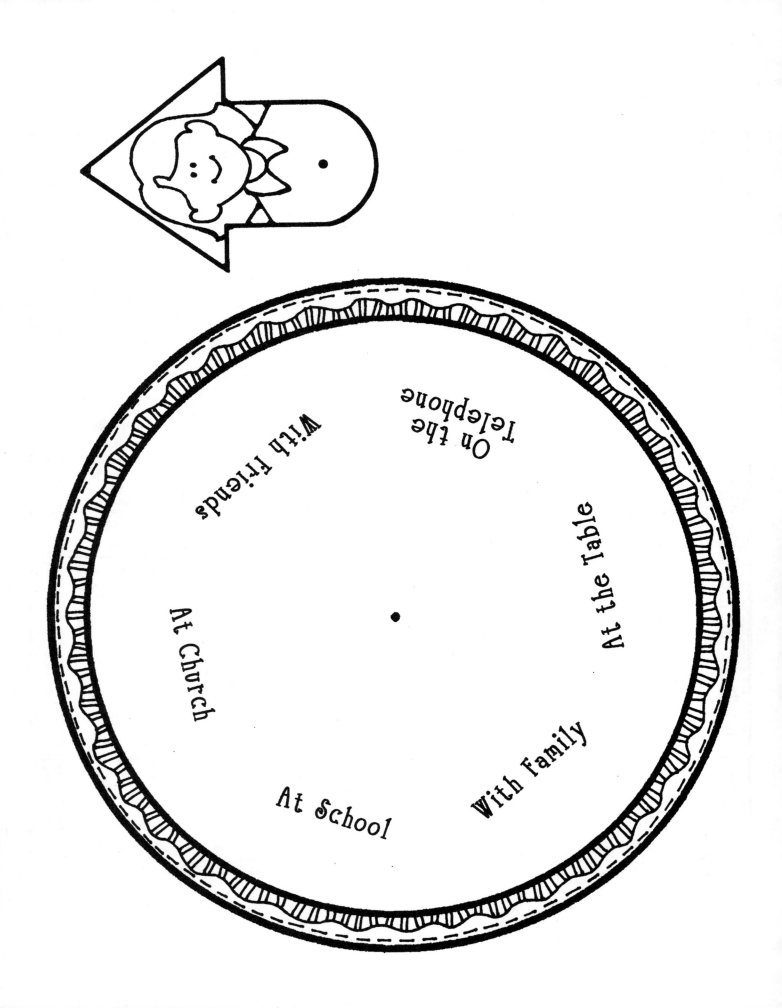

With Friends

On the
Telephone

At the Table

At Church

With Family

At School

| With Friends | At School | Telephone |
|---|---|---|
| Your friend is telling you something about themselves and you are thinking about something else. | Your teacher is explaining an important subject and you have a question. | You are talking on the phone, but your mother has an important call she needs to make. |
| **At School** | **With Family** | **Telephone** |
| You bump against someone in the hall, or you need to pass someone. | You want someone to take out the garbage. | You are talking and another call comes in. |
| **With Family** | **At the Table** | **Telephone** |
| You must interrupt someone who is having a conversation. | You want someone to pass the food to you. | You call someone who doesn't know who you are. |
| **At the Table** | **At the Table** | **Telephone** |
| You are eating at a friend's house and they serve you something you do not like. | You need to place your napkin somewhere. | Your friend calls while you are eating or doing homework. |
| **With Friends** | **At Church** | **Telephone** |
| Someone gives you a gift and you don't like it. | Someone is talking and you want to say something. | You answer the phone, but it is for your sister who is not home. |
| **With Family** | **At the Table** | **With Family** |
| Someone does something nice for you. | You want to say something but your mouth is full of food. | You offended your mother. |
| **With Family** | **At the Table** | **At Church** |
| Your sister shares something with you. | You would like a second serving of food that is out of reach. | Your classmate gave a good talk. |
| **With Friends** | **With Friends** | **With Friends** |
| You want to borrow your friend's clothes. | Your friends visit your home and they are hungry. | The activity you are doing is boring but others are having fun. |
| **At School** | **With Family** | **At the Table** |
| You want to invite a friend to a party and someone you are not inviting is with them. | Your sister's diary was left out on her bed and she is gone. | You are through eating and ready to leave the table. |

For a ROYAL experience, come to Activity Days!

Date: _____

Time: _____

Place: _____

## Serving Others  Goal 7

## Service Activity: We Can Serve Together

**ACTIVITY:** *Plan and hold a parent-child activity, such as a dinner, picnic, hike, day trip, or service project.*

### Once Upon a Time:
### King and Queen for a Day (Senior Spotlight)

Obtain, color, and cut out the *King and Queen for a Day Crown* (shown right), *Once Upon a Time Spot-light Senior Spotlight* (shown left), and a *Good Old Days Bingo Game* board for each player (shown right).

1. Ahead of time, take your parents to visit a chosen senior and interview them, filling in the *Once Upon a Time Spotlight*. Write down things you will say when you crown them king or queen for a day (see #5 below).

2. Invite the senior to your group celebration. See also *Seniors Who Can't Get Out* (below).

3. If you can find old-fashioned items to bring you could display them and have seniors tell about them during the celebrations.

4. Prepare a nice meal and set a table (displaying old-fashioned pictures and things) where you, your senior guest, and your parents can sit around and visit.

5. Play the *Good Old Days Bingo Game* with seniors (see instruction page for rules).

6. Spotlight the seniors one at a time by crowning them with the *King* or *Queen for a Day Crown*, saying, "I crown you Queen Hanna or King Charles," saying their name. Then read their *Once Upon a Time Spotlight*.

**Seniors Who Can't Get Out:** Be sure to visit the seniors in your ward who can't attend the celebration by bringing them treats and spotlight them individually. Ahead of time have someone who knows them help you fill out the *Once Upon a Time Spotlight*. Then you can visit them individually to honor them.

Attach to B

A

Queen for a Day!

Attach to A

B

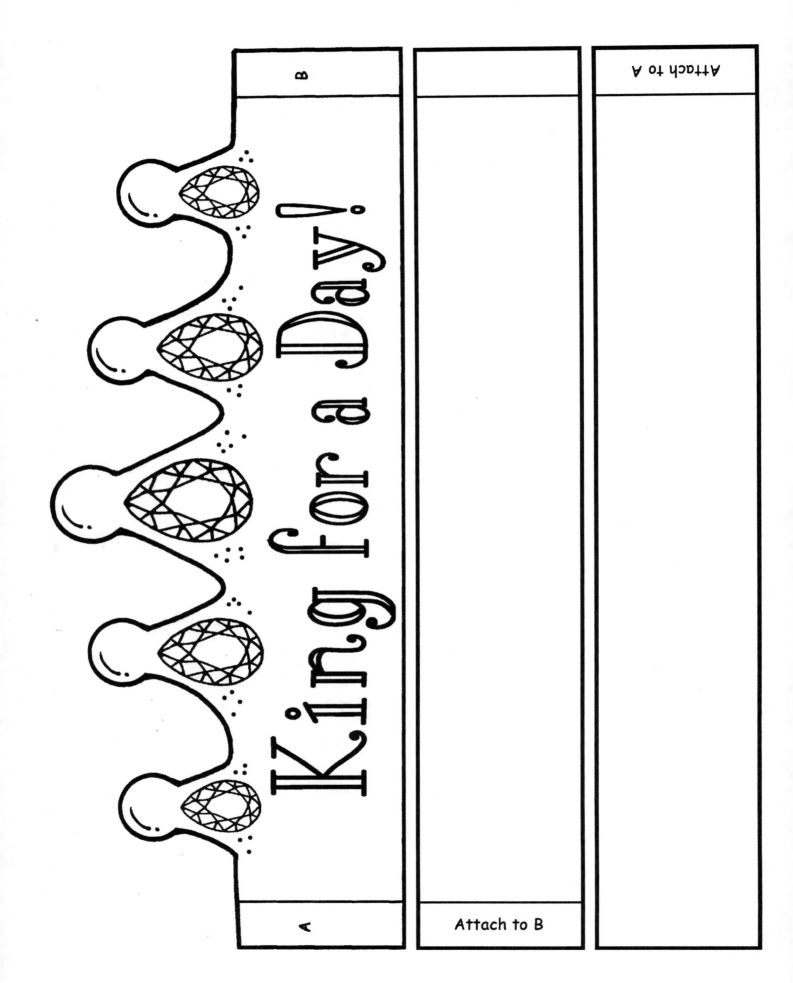

B

King for a Day!

A

Attach to B

Attach to A

# Good Old Days Bingo

**To Make:** Cut out the calling cards below and place in a container.

**Rules:** Give out a bingo card to each player (up to 8 players). Give each person 25 buttons or pennies for markers. Players mark the FREE square with a marker to begin. Have a caller draw a calling card from a container and call out the memory from the good old days, e.g., "hat pin." The players find the word on their card and place the marker. The player who covers a row left and right, up and down, or diagonally wins.

**Treats:** Give old-fashioned treats to winners, e.g., Starlite mints, butter mints, Hershey's chocolate bar, or a lollipop.

| Model T Ford | Baby Buggy | Three Stooges |
| --- | --- | --- |
| Horse and Buggy | Sock Hop | Kick-the-Can |
| Washboard | Icehouse | Lye Soap |
| Wringer Washer | Hat Pin | Black-and-White TV |
| Pocket Watch | Soda Fountain | Garter Belt |
| Silent Movies | Burma Shave | Clothesline |
| Edsel | Little Orphan Annie | Rumble Seat |
| Beehive Hairdo | Corset | Pot-Bellied Stove |
| Radio Shows | Record Player | |
| Newsreels | Carbon Paper | |

# Good Old Days Bingo #1

| | | | | |
|---|---|---|---|---|
| Beehive Hairdo | Soda Fountain | Pot-bellied Stove | Model T Ford | Pocket Watch |
| News-reels | Little Orphan Annie | Lye Soap | Hat Pin | Clothes-line |
| Garter Belt | Horse and Buggy | FREE | Burma Shave | Wash-board |
| Corset | Ice-house | Record Player | Wringer Washer | Rumble Seat |
| Black-&-White T.V. | Carbon Paper | Radio Shows | Silent Movies | Three Stooges |

# Good Old Days Bingo #2

| | | | | |
|---|---|---|---|---|
| Little Orphan Annie | Garter Belt | Ice-house | Soda Fountain | Record Player |
| Black-&-White T.V. | Radio Shows | Silent Movies | Horse and Buggy | Edsel |
| Pot-bellied Stove | Pocket Watch | FREE | Hat Pin | News-reels |
| Beehive Hairdo | Carbon Paper | Wringer Washer | Baby Buggy | Model T Ford |
| Corset | Wash-board | Lye Soap | Three Stooges | Burma Shave |

| Kick-the-Can | Three Stooges | Soda Fountain | Garter Belt | Record Player |
|---|---|---|---|---|
| Carbon Paper | Hat Pin | Pocket Watch | Lye Soap | Black-&-White T.V. |
| Burma Shave | Silent Movies | FREE | Baby Buggy | News-reels |
| Horse and Buggy | Corset | Wringer Washer | Rumble Seat | Ice-house |
| Edsel | Model T Ford | Beehive Hairdo | Radio Shows | Wash-board |

| Three Stooges | Soda Fountain | Beehive Hairdo | Lye Soap | Carbon Paper |
|---|---|---|---|---|
| Baby Buggy | Record Player | Hat Pin | Rumble Seat | Corset |
| News-reels | Ice-house | FREE | Black-&-White T.V. | Radio Shows |
| Wash-board | Pot-bellied Stove | Burma Shave | Silent Movies | Edsel |
| Kick-the-Can | Model T Ford | Horse and Buggy | Garter Belt | Pocket Watch |

# Good Old Days Bingo #5

| Corset | News-reels | Pocket Watch | Carbon Paper | Black-&-White T.V. |
|---|---|---|---|---|
| Pot-bellied Stove | Burma Shave | Horse and Buggy | Rumble Seat | Pocket Watch |
| Silent Movies | Model T Ford | FREE | Record Player | Beehive Hairdo |
| Wash-board | Baby Buggy | Garter Belt | Lye Soap | Radio Shows |
| Soda Fountain | Hat Pin | Wringer Washer | Little Orphan Annie | Three Stooges |

# Good Old Days Bingo #6

| Black-&-White T.V. | Edsel | Little Orphan Annie | Silent Movies | Record Player |
|---|---|---|---|---|
| Pocket Watch | Rumble Seat | Radio Shows | Model T Ford | Baby Buggy |
| Hat Pin | News-reels | FREE | Wash-board | Garter Belt |
| Corset | Lye Soap | Horse and Buggy | Burma Shave | Pot-bellied Stove |
| Pocket Watch | Beehive Hairdo | Carbon Paper | Three Stooges | Soda Fountain |

## Good Old Days #8 — Bingo

| Newsreels | Rumble Seat | Pocket Watch | Sock Hop | Pot-bellied Stove |
|---|---|---|---|---|
| Pocket Watch | Ice-house | Soda Fountain | Horse and Buggy | Wringer Washer |
| Silent Movies | Model T Ford | FREE | Baby Buggy | Record Player |
| Little Orphan Annie | Edsel | Washboard | Lye Soap | Radio Shows |
| Beehive Hairdo | Three Stooges | Burma Shave | Garter Belt | Hat Pin |

## Good Old Days #7 — Bingo

| Ice-house | Soda Fountain | Hat Pin | Horse and Buggy | Pocket Watch |
|---|---|---|---|---|
| Wringer Washer | Lye Soap | Corset | Beehive Hairdo | Black-&-White T.V. |
| Radio Shows | Carbon Paper | FREE | Kick-the-Can | Washboard |
| Burma Shave | Silent Movies | Three Stooges | Garter Belt | Pot-bellied Stove |
| Rumble Seat | Model T Ford | Record Player | Newsreels | Little Orphan Annie |

## Serving Others  Goal 8

### Good Citizen: My Actions Affect Others

**ACTIVITY 1:** *Read the twelfth article of faith.*

**ACTIVITY 2:** *Discuss what it means to be a good citizen and how your actions can affect others.*

### Action and Reaction
### (Missing Service Match Game)

1. Obtain, color, and cut out the *Action and Reaction Missing Card Match* Game cards (shown right).

2. Talk about what it means to be a good citizen to build up your community and your country. What can you do to be a good citizen? What can you contribute to make your world better?

*To Play:*

1. Cut the cards in half where indicated. Put the matching halves together and talk about each action and what the reaction is (how your actions affect others).

2. Mix up the card halves and turn them facedown. Divide into teams and take turns turning the cards over to make a match, e.g., "Donate a toy to a charity," matches with "Blesses the life of a needy child." The team with the most cards wins!

Shovel the walk...

Visit a historical museum or site of interest.

MAP

Pick up garbage in public places.

Others can enjoy beautiful parks and roadsides.

Donate a toy to a local charity.

Blesses the life of a needy child.

Volunteer at a nearby homeless shelter.

Blesses those who need a helping hand.

Recycle paper, plastic, and aluminum.

Reduces the size of the landfills.

Donate a toy to a local charity.

Blesses the life of a needy child.

Plant a tree.

Makes the community beautiful.

Obey traffic laws while riding my bike.

Keeps myself and others safe.

Pick up garbage in public places.

Others can enjoy beautiful parks and roadsides.

Be considerate of wildlife and animal habitat.

Protects our natural surroundings.

Learn to care for and correctly display the flag.

Encourages patriotism and respect for the flag.

Get yourself to Activity Days!

Date:

Time:

Place:

## Serving Others Goal 9

## Planning: I Will Help Plan an Activity

**ACTIVITY:** *Help your Primary leaders plan and carry out an upcoming quarterly activity.*

### Drive-in Movie (Primary Party)

1. Make this "Drive-in Movie" theme fun, holding it inside the church.
2. Obtain, color, and cut out the *Drive-in Movie Party Plans* and *Red-Light, Green-Light Stop-and-Go Signs* (shown right).
3. Make your own invitation, copying the car image (shown right).
4. Have children bring their own box. Have them decorate their box using the car license plate, wheels and headlights.
5. Children can sit in the box to watch a short, 15-minute movie or cartoons.
6. Play games before the movie.

**Game 1—Car Relay Rally:**
Divide children into teams. At "go," have two from each team race across a room with a child in the car and an older child behind them, pushing them to the finish line. The first to arrive receives a point for their team.

**Game 2—Red Light, Green Light:** To make the signs, mount them on large wooden craft sticks (shown left). Have a child with both signs in their hand hold one sign up at a time as children race their car (pushing it from behind) towards the goal line. Children can race while the "Go" sign is up, but must stop when the "Stop" sign goes up. If they keep moving after the stop sign is up, they have to go back to start.

7. Sing "Wheels on the Car" (instead of "Wheels on the Bus").
8. Make treats children can enjoy while watching the movie. You might pack a sack lunch for each child. *Ideas:* popcorn balls · gummy Lifesaver wheels · Rice Krispies squares · fruit leather · trail mix · pretzels · cookies · string licorice · granola bar · animal crackers · water

Come and be a particip"ant" at Activity Days!

Date: _____

Time: _____

Place: _____

## Serving Others  Goal 10

### FAITHFUL SERV"ANT"
#### Service Planner

WHO I want to serve: _____

WHY I want to serve: _____
_____
_____

WHAT I want to do: _____
_____
_____

WHERE I will go: _____
_____

WHEN I will serve: _____
_____
_____

## Service: I Will Be a Serv"ant"

**ACTIVITY:** *Plan and complete your own activity to serve others.*

### Faithful Serv"ant" (Service Planner)

If we study an ant we would realize they are one of the most industrious insects. They are always working to make life better. We too can be faithful Serv"ants" and serve others.

1. Obtain and color the *Faithful Serv"ant" Project Planner* (shown right).

2. Answer the questions on the planner, e.g., "who," "what," etc. to plan your service project. Then complete the service project.

# FAiTHFUL SERVANT"
## Service Planner

WHO I want to serve: _____
_____

WHY I want to serve: _____
_____
_____
_____

WHAT I want to do: _____
_____
_____
_____
_____

WHERE I will go: _____
_____

WHEN I will serve: _____
_____

## 1. SERVICE: Service Helps My Faith Grow Stronger

(Service Is in Style Cookies). Have girls help cut out 4" sugar cookies into fashion shapes (see ideas underlined below). Then bake, frost, and decorate.

**Thoughts:** As you eat cookies, talk about these *Fashionable Ways to Serve*:

• Top off your day with prayer and remember those that need special blessings.
• Skirt pride and selfishness and forget yourself and listen to others.
• Polish your talents and share with others what your fingers can do.
• Curl up in a chair with a child and read them a good book.
• Hats off to Mom for all she does; give her a day off household chores.
• *Brush* up your pearly whites and share your smile with the lonely.
• You can be fashionable without spending a dime and serve with a smile time after time (see 2 Corinthians 9:7).
• Get your socks to hop to it and serve by running an errand.
• Cinch up your belt for fast Sunday and prepare the after-fast meal ahead of time.
• Slip into a new habit and serve someone new each week.
• Roll up your sleeves and do an extra batch of dishes.
• Boot yourself out of bed and make your family a surprise breakfast.

## 2. GRATITUDE: I Will Express Appreciation

(Grateful Heart Bread). Make a batch of bread dough, following a simple recipe but adding ½ teaspoon red food coloring and 3/4 cup sugar into dough before adding the flour. Form raised bread dough into heart shapes. Frost with a red frosting glaze (add 3 drops red food coloring and 2-3 tablespoons canned milk to a carton of vanilla frosting).

**Thought:** As girls enjoy their heart-shaped bread, talk about things that have happened to them this past month that have warmed their heart.

## 3. CHARACTER: I Will Develop Sweet-Spirit Qualities

(Kindness Cookies). Make a batch of sugar cookies and take to a girl who may have been offended somehow or who needs to be invited to Activity Days. The girls will know who it can be. *Option:* They could sit on the doorstep with this girl and share some of the cookies they made as they talk, giving her a separate plate wrapped up especially for her.

## 4. THOUGHTFUL CHEF: I Will Create Nutritious Meals

(Ants on a Log). Spread sugarless peanut butter into a 4" piece of celery and top with 4-5 raisins. Tell girls that many nutritious snacks like this one will only take a minute to prepare.

**Thought:** Brainstorm easy-to-fix snacks, e.g., peanut butter and banana sandwich, apples and peanut butter (rather than caramel), vegetables with ranch dip, fruit with yogurt dip, melt cheese on whole wheat tortillas, cut out cheese slices or bologna into face shapes.

## 5. CHILD CARE: Learn Babysitting Basics

**(Barnyard Bread Sticks).**

Form purchased bread-stick dough or homemade raised dough into animal shapes and bake according to directions. Decorate bread sticks by squirting processed cheese from the can to create barnyard animals. Add candies or vegetables to help decorate. *Thought:* Review the *Babysitting Barnyard Basics* as you eat.

## 6. MANNERS: I Will Practice Good Manners and Courtesy

**(Charming Manners Charm Bracelet).** Supply five or more gummy or hard Lifesaver candies and string licorice for girls to make a *Charming Manners Charm Bracelet*. Thread the candies onto the licorice and tie. *Thought:* Talk about each charm treat as a manner they wish to develop in the coming week. As they practice the manner they can eat the charm.

## 7. SERVICE: We Can Serve Together

**(King and Queen Crown Cookie).** Make a crown-shaped sugar cookie; bake, frost, and top it with candy jewels. Share cookies with seniors at your service activity. These could be served when girls plan the service activity. When they add candy jewels on the crown have them think of the jewels they will be receiving on their heavenly crown for serving others.

## 8. GOOD CITIZEN: My Actions Affect Others

**(Circle of Love Cinnamon Rolls)** Make or purchase cinnamon rolls.

*Thought:* As you eat, talk about the circle of love and influence we have on others that is never ending. Name ways we can include others in our circle of love. Talk about Abraham and how he included Lot into his circle of love (see lesson 10 attention activity on page 39 in the *Primary 6—Old Testament Manual*).

## 9. PLANNING: I Will Help Plan an Activity

**(Growing Imagination Marshmallows).** Tell girls that our imaginations can grow like marshmallows expanding in the oven if we work at it. Place a marshmallow on a plate and pop it into the microwave oven to warm up and watch it grow. Have girls use their imaginations to create marshmallow treats. Have supplies on hand to help girls create.

***Growing Imagination Ideas:*** (1) Beatle Bug Motor Car: Place gumdrops or gummy Lifesavers candies on the sides of a marshmallow. Cook 10 seconds to watch it grow into a funny car shape. (2) Moon Crater: Cut a large marshmallow in half and press the sticky side into decorator candies. Place both halves in the microwave for 10 seconds. (3) Space Ship: Pierce four holes in the sides of a large marshmallow and push shelled peanuts into holes. Cook 20 seconds.

## 10. SERVICE: I Will Be a Serv"ant"

**(Ant Farm Fudge).** Melt a bag of sweetened chocolate chips, $\frac{1}{2}$ can of sweetened and condensed milk, and $\frac{1}{2}$ teaspoon vanilla in the microwave for 2 minutes. Stir, and cook another minute or two until melted. When cool, butter fingers and roll fudge into balls. Press down and top with chocolate-covered or plain raisins (ants). Tell girls that ants are farming all day, working hard to serve. We too can be like the industrious ants.

Sure hope you "coin" come to Activity Days!

Date: _____
Time: _____
Place: _____

Developing Talents  Goal 1    Budgeting: I Will Pay My Tithing and Save My Money

**ACTIVITY 1:** *Learn how to budget and save money. Pay your tithing and begin saving for an education.*

### My Cash Commitment (Envelopes)

1. Obtain, color, and cut out the *My Cash Commitment Envelope* labels (shown right). Glue labels on envelopes.
2. Write on the labels the percentage of money you will put in each envelope each time you divide your money, e.g., 10% tithing, 30% education, 20% long-term savings (write in goal), 20% short-term savings, 20% spending.
3. Try to pay tithing the Sunday after being paid. If savings amounts are growing, deposit money in a savings account for safety.

### Mind Your Money (Game)

Obtain, color, and cut out the
*Mind Your Money Game* (shown left), and play the game (see rules).

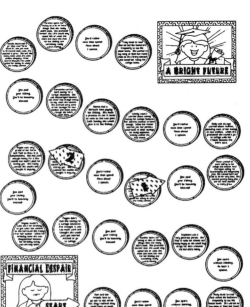

**ACTIVITY 2:** *Discuss why it is important to faithfully pay our tithing and how Heavenly Father blesses us when we do (3 Nephi 24:10-11).*

### Windows of Heaven (Scripture Chase)

1. Obtain, color, and cut out a set of *Windows of Heaven Scripture Chase* cards (shown right).
2. Talk about how the Lord has promised to bless us as we faithfully pay tithing. Read Malachi 3:10 ("open the windows of heaven, and pour you out a blessing, that there shall not be room enough to receive it").

*Scripture Chase:* Divide into teams. Take turns drawing a card and both teams race to find the scripture. The first team to find it places it in their scriptures to mark their place and earns a point. Take turns reading the scriptures found.

# My Cash Commitment

## SHORT-TERM SAVINGS

Things of value are not quickly obtained. I commit to saving for the following:

_____

%

# My Cash Commitment

## SPENDING

Money is a joy when used wisely. Before spending think twice; knowing that once it is gone, it will never return.

%

**Mind Your Money Game:** Discover ways to "a bright future." So you won't end up in "financial despair," save your money for the things that will really make a difference. This game will help you learn to make good money choices now so you can have a jump-start on your future. You can save for items such as: college tuition, books, car, gasoline, car repair, car insurance, rent, food, clothing, entertainment.

*Game Rules:* (1) Divide into two teams, giving each team an arrow marker (team 1 or team 2), placing markers at the START. (2) Teams take turns rolling a die to determine the number of moves on the path.
(3) Throw the die to determine who moves first (highest number starts).
(4) First team to play rolls the die and moves along the path the number of spaces rolled. (5) Player reads an action on the coin she lands on. Player decides if the action is "minding your money" or if it is "misusing your money." (6) Player moves their arrow toward the FUTURE if the situation on the coin is a "minding your money" action, or towards START if it is a "misusing your money" action. This is the direction they will travel on their next turn (for one turn only) unless the choice causes them to change directions. If they get all the way to START they can begin again.

# My Cash Commitment
## TITHING

I am grateful to the Lord for all His blessings. I will glady do my part to help build the kingdom of God.

**10%**

# My Cash Commitment
## EDUCATION

Educating myself is my greatest investment. I commit to preparing for my future by saving for school.

**%**

# My Cash Commitment
## LONG-TERM SAVINGS

Things of value are not quickly obtained. I commit to saving for the following:

_____

**%**

Stephanie was a very generous person. She liked to make her friends and family happy, so she would buy things for them whenever she had extra money.

Sally was always worried about fashion, spending most of her money on new clothes. When she graduated she couldn't go to college with her friends because she hadn't saved.

Regan was very proud of her horse and liked to show it in competitions. She had just enough money for a new saddle but hadn't paid her tithing yet. She really wanted the saddle and bought it anyway.

Megan didn't feel like saving for a college education. She thought it was too much work and thought she would just get married instead of go to college.

Wendy wasn't worried about saving money for college because her parents seemed to have enough. When her father lost his job, her parents used most of thier savings for living expenses. Wendy wished she had saved.

Samantha worked hard saving for a college education. She was discouraged because she never had enough money to buy what she wanted. She started using some of her savings for new clothes and shoes even though she didn't need them.

Angela couldn't wait until her birthday to get what she wanted, so she borrowed the money from her mother. When her birthday came she was disappointed because her birthday money was already spent.

You paid your tithing. You'll be heavenly blessed!

You paid your tithing. You'll be heavenly blessed!

Keri and her friends love to eat out often, but they realized they could have as much fun and save money by cooking a meal together.

Rosa really liked to grow and sell flowers. She saved the extra cash she earned until the next season so she could buy more seeds. Each year her small business grew.

Peggy loved the clothes in the expensive stores, but knew she couldn't afford then and still have money for things she needed. Instead, she saved money by shopping at less expensive stores.

Mindy loved to read and visited the bookstore frequently to see the latest books. She wanted to buy many of them but found them at the library instead and saved her money for college books.

Fran's aunt was going to college and Fran asked her how much things cost. Then Fran started saving her money so she would be ready when that day came.

Wanda decorated a jar that read "think about it," and put cash in the bottle each week. She watched it grow. She left the money home when she went window shopping. After careful thought she would spend her money on what she really wanted.

Candice spent her money on a lot of little things that she really didn't need. She promised herself that she would only spend 20% of what she made and save the rest for her tithing and something really worth having.

Hanna had a difficult time paying her tithing. She made a promise to set it aside as soon as she was paid. Each Sunday she would give it to the bishop.

Karen wanted to start adding to her college and mission fund. She began asking for housekeeping and babysitting jobs. She worked hard and tried to do her very best. She started getting many jobs and her fund started to really grow.

You'd rather save than spend! Move ahead 2 spaces.

You spent without thinking. Go back 3 spaces.

You'd rather save than spend! Move ahead 2 spaces.

You'd rather save than spend! Move ahead 2 spaces.

You spent without thinking. Go back 3 spaces.

You paid your tithing. You'll be heavenly blessed!

You'd rather save than spend! Move ahead 2 spaces.

You paid your tithing. You'll be heavenly blessed!

You paid your tithing. You'll be heavenly blessed!

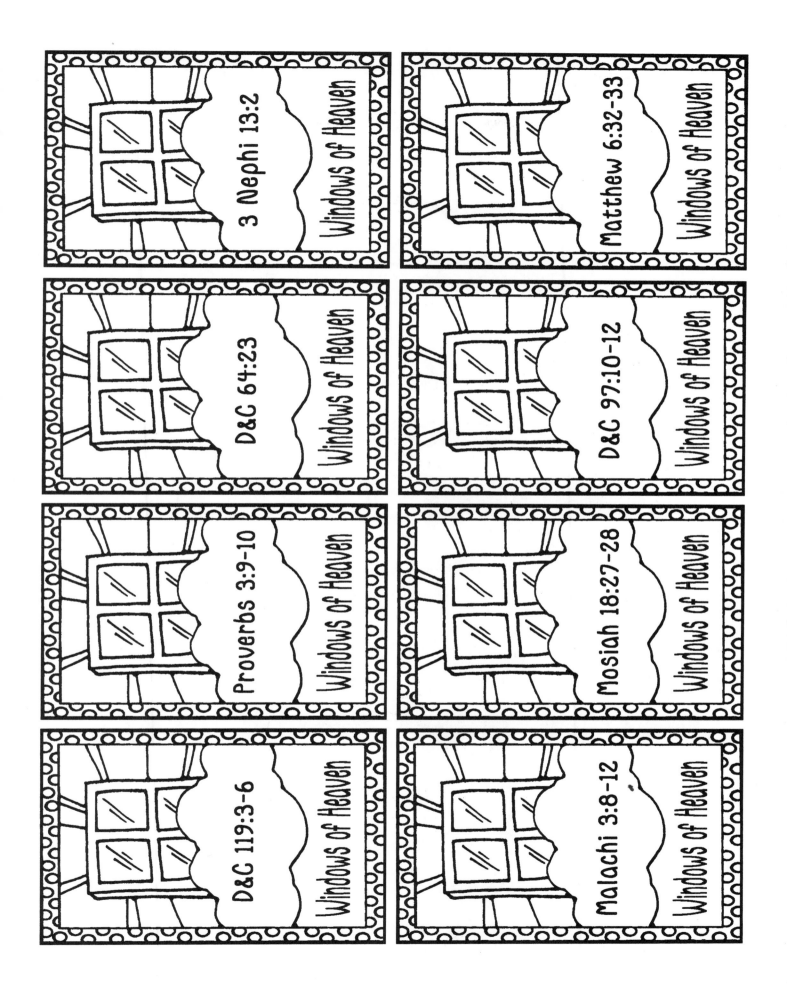

Windows of Heaven — 3 Nephi 13:2

Windows of Heaven — Matthew 6:32-33

Windows of Heaven — D&C 64:23

Windows of Heaven — D&C 97:10-12

Windows of Heaven — Proverbs 3:9-10

Windows of Heaven — Mosiah 18:27-28

Windows of Heaven — D&C 119:3-6

Windows of Heaven — Malachi 3:8-12

On a good note,
we want you at
Activity Days!

Date:

Time:

Place:

## Developing Talents  Goal 2

## Talents: I Will Prepare to Serve Others

**ACTIVITY 1:** *Learn to sing, play, or lead a song from the "Children's Songbook." Teach or share the song in a family home evening or Primary.*

### "Hum Your Favorite Hymn" (Singing Face Wheel)

1. Obtain, color, and cut out the " *Hum Your Favorite Hymn" Singing Face* visual (shown right). Cut out the window on top of the head. Attach part A wheel to part B face with a paper fastener (metal brad). Obtain a copy of the " *Hum Your Favorite Hymn,"* in the *Children's Songbook*, p. 152.
2. Use the visual to teach the song by turning the wheel and showing the picture through the window.
3. When you come to the chorus, turn the wheel back around to matching visuals.
4. See p. 301 in the *Children's Songbook* to lead *"Hum Your Favorite Hymn"* using the 2/4 beat pattern.

**ACTIVITY 2:** *Discuss how developing talents helps prepare us for service to Heavenly Father and others.*

### Lightning and Thunder (Talent Brainstorm)

Obtain, color, and cut out the *Lightning and Thunder Talent Brainstorm* cards (shown left) and place cards in a container.

*Brainstorm:* You have to be as quick as a bolt of lightning or clap of thunder to think up these talents. Divide into two teams and take turns drawing a talent card from the container. The team drawing the card has 10 seconds to look at the image on the card and think of a talent that matches the image and then tell how that talent benefits others. If they can't, the other team has 10 seconds to do so to earn the point.

Cut Out

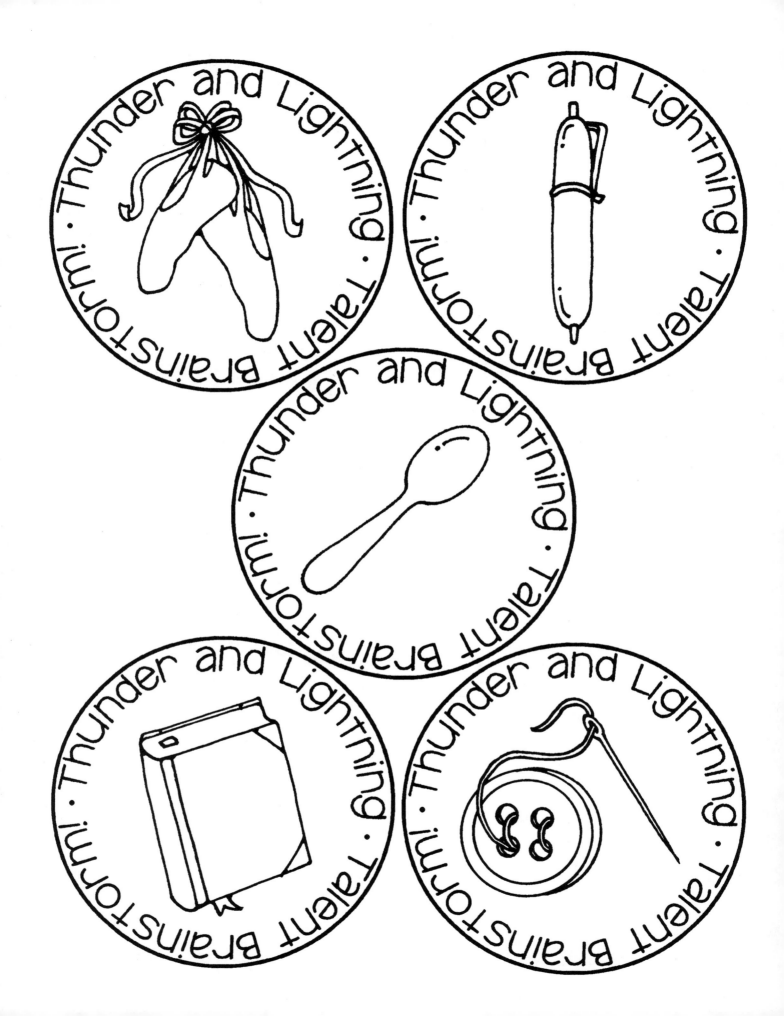

Come to an
out-of-this-world
Activity Days!

Date: _____

Time: _____

Place: _____

## Developing Talents  Goal 3

## Writing: I Can Teach Gospel Principles

**ACTIVITY 1:** *Write a poem, story, or short play that teaches a principle of the gospel or is about Heavenly Father's creations.*

### My Writing Creation (Notebook)

Obtain and color the *Writing Creation Notebook* (shown right). Staple writing pages to the cover, write your name on the front, and write inside as detailed above.

Come and get artsy-smartsy at Activity Days!

Date: _____

Time: _____

Place: _____

## Developing Talents  Goal 4

## Crafts: I Can Create Many Works of Art

**ACTIVITY:** *Make an item from wood, metal, fabric, or other material, or draw, paint, or sculpt a piece of art. Display your finished work for others to see.*

### Nature Prints
### (Calendar, Card, and Picture Frame)

(1) Obtain and cut out the *Nature Prints Calendar, Card, and Envelope* patterns (shown right). (2) Make a calendar, card, and envelope following the ideas below and on the calendar page. (3) Purchase a paintable picture frame and decorate as detailed below.

*Ideas:* 1) Find items to decorate these projects, e.g., leaves, apple halves, tiny shells or twigs. Create a pattern using items. 2) Using a leaf or apple slice, paint one side of the leaf or apple and press it onto the paper to make a print. Lay another piece of paper on top to press the ink onto your project (keeping hands clean). 3) Glue on tiny shells or twigs.

### Rock Fun
### (Tic-Tac-Toe Game and Rock Creations)

Obtain, color, cut out, and laminate the *Tic-Tac-Toe Game Board* (shown right).

**Tic-Tac-Toe Game Board:** Find small rocks. Paint 10 rocks to fit in squares and paint five one color and five another color. Use as markers to play the game. *Rules:* Take turns placing a rock on the board. The first player to place three rocks in a straight or diagonal line wins.

**Rock Creations:** Use your imagination to paint: 1) a medium-sized rock to create a prayer rock to place under a pillow to remind someone to say prayers, 2) a small or medium-sized rock to create a pet rock—painting an animal or insect, 3) a larger rock to create a doorstop or the decorate a garden.

**To Create Calendar:**
1. Decorate an 8 1/2" x 11" or larger sheet of paper.
2. Cut out calendar (shown below) and spray the back with spray-on adhesive and mount it on the page.
3. Bind calendar using staples or hole punch and ribbon.

## Calendar Pattern

Month _____ Year _____

| Sunday | Monday | Tuesday | Wednesday | Thursday | Friday | Sunday |
|--------|--------|---------|-----------|----------|--------|--------|
| ☐ | ☐ | ☐ | ☐ | ☐ | ☐ | ☐ |
| ☐ | ☐ | ☐ | ☐ | ☐ | ☐ | ☐ |
| ☐ | ☐ | ☐ | ☐ | ☐ | ☐ | ☐ |
| ☐ | ☐ | ☐ | ☐ | ☐ | ☐ | ☐ |
| ☐ | ☐ | ☐ | ☐ | ☐ | ☐ | ☐ |

# Card Pattern

Center
Fold

Envelope Pattern

From:

To:

# Tic-Tac-Toe Board Pattern

Developing Talents  Goal 5        Cultural Arts: I Will Learn to Appreciate the Arts

**ACTIVITY:** *Visit an art museum or attend a concert, play, or other cultural event. Share your experiences with your family or activity day group.*

### I Love the Cultural Arts! (Frame/Journal)

1. Obtain and color the *I Love the Cultural Arts Frame/Journal* (shown right).

2. Review the 13th Article of Faith and think of ways you can add to your life and to the lives of others through cultural arts. Many of these are found in the frame (shown right).

2. Attend a cultural event. Then use the *Cultural Arts! Frame/Journal* to record your experiences and/or display photos of a cultural event you attended.

### Cultural Art Activity Ideas:

• **Museum Show-and-Tell:** At a museum, divide your group into two groups to scope out the museum in sections. Then get together and show the other group what you discovered, having several girls act as the tour guides for their portion of the museum.  Take photos to place on the *I Love Cultural Arts!* frame/journal page (above) and write about your findings and experience.

• **Teach Dance Steps:** Have someone come and teach the basics: ballet, western swing, line dancing, square dancing, folk dance, ballroom, disco, break dancing, and more.

• **Have a Casual Talent Night:** Find an interest or talent from each girl to spotlight. Have girls share their talents, e.g., piano, flute, guitar, craft skill, cooking demos, singing, scrapbooks, crafts.  Display items made and have them tell about their hobbies and interests and how they got started.

• **Old Movie Night:** Bring a favorite old movie to share or enjoy an animated movie together.

• **Go to a local play.**

• **Put on a play for the next ward party.**

I ♥ the Cultural Arts!

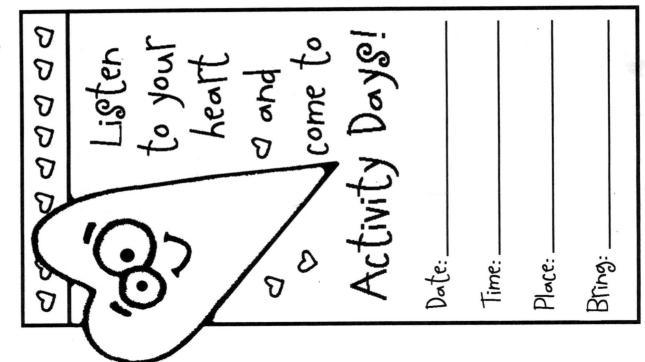

Date: _____

Time: _____

Place: _____

Bring: _____

## Developing Talents  Goal 6        Education: I Will Improve My Study Habits

**ACTIVITY 1:** *Read D&C 88:118. Discuss what it means to "seek learning, even by study and also by faith."*

### "Bee" Smart and Read with All Your Heart (Book Cover)

1. Obtain, color, and cut out the *"Bee" Smart and Read with All Your Heart Book Cover* glue-on stickers (shown right).

2. Using a brown grocery bag, make a book cover by laying the back cover of your reading book on paper and cutting paper 3" wider than book. See instructions on sticker page. This same book cover can be adjusted for larger or smaller books that you are currently reading by folding the flaps to adjust.

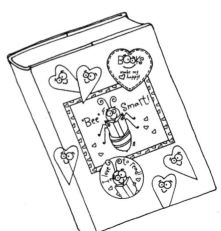

**ACTIVITY 2:** *Improve your personal study habits by doing such things as learning how to choose and read good books or being prepared for school each day.*

### "Bee" Smart (Bookmark—Good Book Reading List)

1. Obtain, color, and cut out the *"Bee" Smart Bookmark—Good Book Reading List* (shown right).

2. You can improve your study habits by choosing books from this list to read, and following the "Bee" Smart hints.

### Smart Bees and Hearts (Checkers)

1. Obtain, color, and cut out the *Smart Bees and Hearts Checkers Game* (shown left). See game rules on the checkerboard page to play.

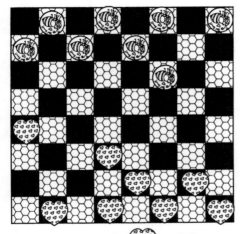

How to fold and put
on your book cover:

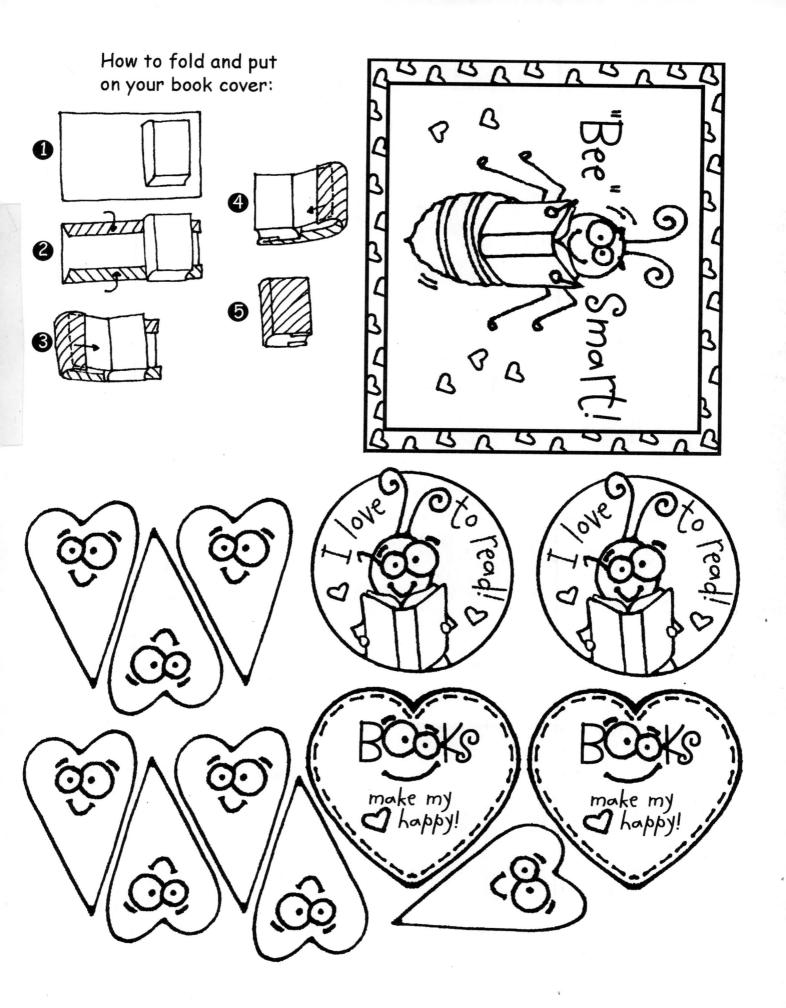

## "Bee" Smart Hints

- Take a planner to school and jot down all assignments.
- Go with the attitude to listen and learn.
- Be sure to get plenty of rest the night before.
- Eat right so your mind will be alert.
- Exercise to avoid fatigue.
- Have a study spot without TV, radio, or any interruptions.
- Complete the most important assignments first.
- Pray before you study.

## Read with All Your Heart!

### Great Book List:

Alice in Wonderland
All Creatures Great & Small
Anne of Green Gables
Beauty and the Beast
Betsy and Tacy
Brighty of the Grand Canyon
Christmas Carol
Chronicles of Narnia
Girl of the Limberlost
Heidi
Little House on the Prarie
Little Princess
Little Women
Mary Poppins
Pollyanna
Rebecca of Sunnybrook Farms
Secret Garden
Where the Red Fern Grows
Wrinkle in Time

## "Bee" Smart Hints

- Take a planner to school and jot down all assignments.
- Go with the attitude to listen and learn.
- Be sure to get plenty of rest the night before.
- Eat right so your mind will be alert.
- Exercise to avoid fatigue.
- Have a study spot without TV, radio, or any interruptions.
- Complete the most important assignments first.
- Pray before you study.

## Read with All Your Heart!

### Great Book List:

Alice in Wonderland
All Creatures Great & Small
Anne of Green Gables
Beauty and the Beast
Betsy and Tacy
Brighty of the Grand Canyon
Christmas Carol
Chronicles of Narnia
Girl of the Limberlost
Heidi
Little House on the Prarie
Little Princess
Little Women
Mary Poppins
Pollyanna
Rebecca of Sunnybrook Farms
Secret Garden
Where the Red Fern Grows
Wrinkle in Time

Fold

Fold

# Smart Bees and Hearts (Checkers)

**To Play:** Divide into two teams, giving one team the bee checkers and the other team the heart checkers.

**Rules:** When a team jumps the other player taking a checker or checkers, that player can name one way you can "Bee" Smart found on the bookmark or name their own way they can increase their knowledge. The winning team says together, "Bee" smart and learn with all your heart."

Make 4 copies and cut out. Spray the backs of the checkerboard pieces with spray adhesive. Mount them on cardboard or poster-board backing.

Whirl on over to our next Activity Days!

Date:

Time:

Place:

Developing Talents  Goal 7

**Tornado Timer**
*Quick Housecleaning List*

List the 5 most important things that need to be cleaned today. Set your timer for 5 minutes and quickly, working as fast as you can, complete the first item on the list. When the timer rings, stop! Set your timer again and start on the next item and continue until your list is done!

❶ _____
❷ _____
❸ _____
❹ _____
❺ _____

## Homemaking: I Will Learn to Help at Home

**ACTIVITY:** *List five things you can do to help around the home. Discuss the importance of obeying and honoring your parents and learning how to work.*

### Tornado Timer (Quick Housecleaning List)

1. Obtain and color the *Tornado Timer Quick Housecleaning List* (shown left) and a timer.
2. Do the following routine using a timer to learn how to beat the clock and clean a house in little time. Timing is everything when you have very little time and the house needs cleaning. By using a timer you can go through the house like a tornado and make a clean sweep of everything.

With this list and your timer your can obey your parents and learn how to work.

### How to Clean the House Using the Tornado Timer:

1. Take out your timer and *Tornado Timer Checklist* and list of at least five things you can do to help around the house (ideas below).
2. Practice beating the clock. Test your timer skills by allowing yourself five minutes to work on each of the five things on your list. Set the timer, go like a tornado to the project and work on it. When the timer rings, set the timer again for five minutes and go onto the next task until you have worked on all five.
3. Repeat this process each day, making work into play. Spend more time on things that require a little more effort.

**Tornado Timer Tasks:** iron, make beds, laundry, clean or vacuum floors, dust, put things away (with a place for everything), wash dishes, wash windows, do gardening, plan menus, prepare meals, clean bathrooms, shine mirrors, dust, clean the garage, clean the car, empty garbage, and clean out cupboards, closets, and drawers.

# Tornado Timer

## Quick Housecleaning List

List the 5 most important things that need to be cleaned today. Set your timer for 5 minutes and quickly, working as fast as you can, complete the first item on the list. When the timer rings, stop! Set your timer again and start on the next item and continue until your list is done!

1.
2.
3.
4.
5.

# Tornado Timer

## Quick Housecleaning List

List the 5 most important things that need to be cleaned today. Set your timer for 5 minutes and quickly, working as fast as you can, complete the first item on the list. When the timer rings, stop! Set your timer again and start on the next item and continue until your list is done!

1.
2.
3.
4.
5.

# Tornado Timer

## Quick Housecleaning List

List the 5 most important things that need to be cleaned today. Set your timer for 5 minutes and quickly, working as fast as you can, complete the first item on the list. When the timer rings, stop! Set your timer again and start on the next item and continue until your list is done!

**1** _____

**2** _____

**3** _____

**4** _____

**5** _____

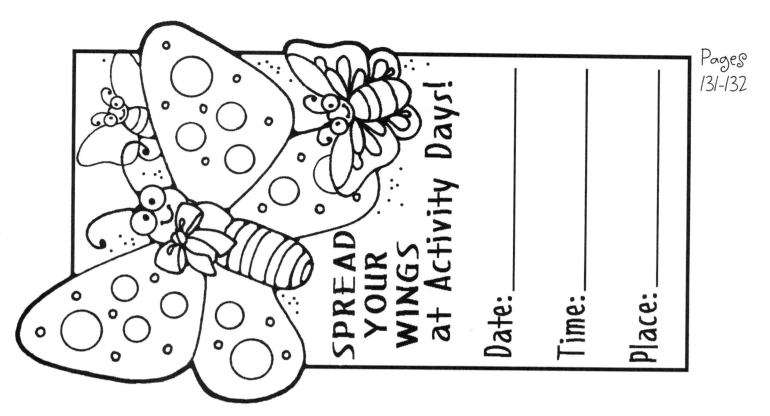

SPREAD YOUR WINGS at Activity Days!

Date: _____

Time: _____

Place: _____

**Developing Talents  Goal 8**         **Physical Fitness: I Will Develop Strength**

**ACTIVITY:** *Plan a physical fitness program for yourself that may include learning to play a sport or game. Participate in the program for one month.*

## Spread My Wings (Exercise Routine)

1. Obtain and color the *Spread My Wings Exercise Routine* butterfly (shown right).
2. Bring you, the butterfly out of your cocoon by writing your goal for physical fitness on the butterfly's belly.
3. Spread Your Wings: For four weeks work on your exercise routine goal (what you plan to do every day) for at least 30 minutes a day. Check off or color the dots for each day (days 1-6) on that week's wing.
*Option:* You could even write on the dots different sports you wish to play or exercises to learn on different days.
*Sports:* soccer, baseball, swimming, jogging, roller blading, tennis, volley ball.
*Exercises:* weight lifting, aerobics, swimming, step, spin, yoga, kick boxing.

4. Take Flight: Go on to the next week (wing) until you have filled in the dots.
*Option:* Laminate the butterfly before writing in your goal. Then you can change the goals next month and place stickers on the dots when you achieve your goal each day.

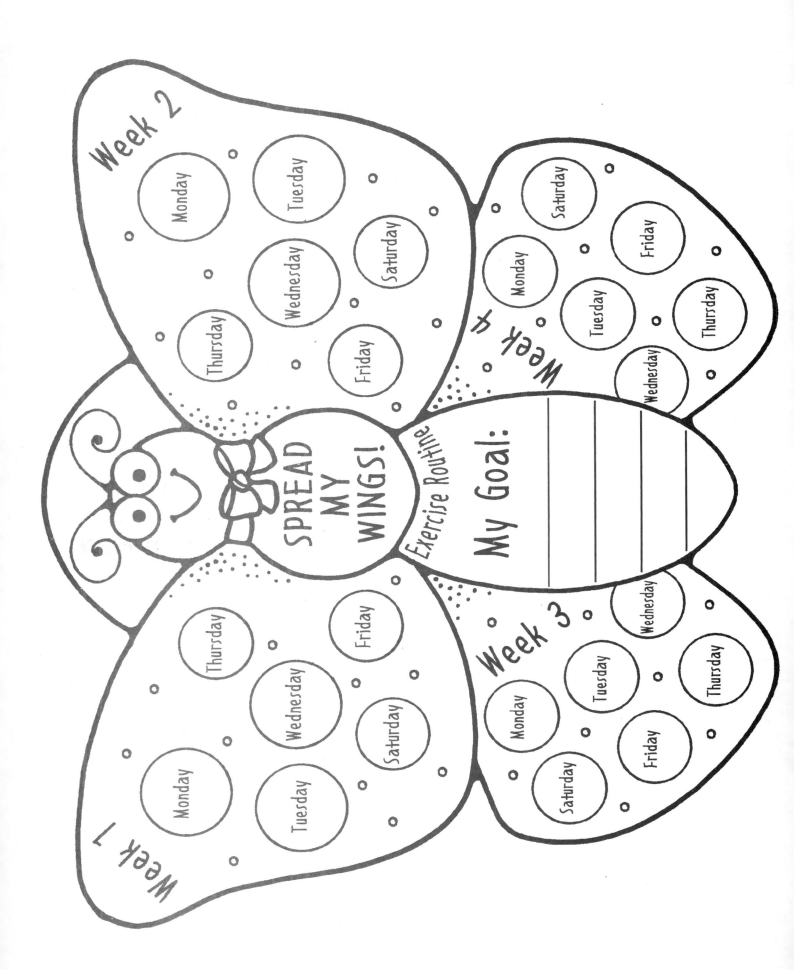

Put a smile on your face at Activity Days!

Date: _____

Time: _____

Place: _____

## Developing Talents Goal 9    Choices: I Will Make Good Choices for My Body

**ACTIVITY:** *Learn about and practice good nutrition, good health, and good grooming, including modest dress.*

### Do I Groan or Glow?
### (Pin the Choices on Groany Joni or Glowy Cloe)

1. Obtain, color, and cut out the *Glowy Cloe* and *Groany Joni Posters* and cards (shown right).

2. Talk about *Groany Joni* who groans and moans because she doesn't feel good physically or with how she is taking care of herself. She feels this way because she doesn't practice good nutrition, good health, good grooming, or modesty. What could she do to change?

3. Talk about *Glowy Cloe* who glows with good health, who radiates because she takes good care of herself and practices good nutrition, good health, good grooming, and modesty.

*To Play:*

1. Divide girls into two teams. Tape the *Glowy Cloe* and *Groany Joni Posters* on the wall next to each other.

2. Line up, having team members take turns drawing a card from the container and placing tape on the back of the card. Decide which action on the card matches which girl, naming either *Glowy Cloe* or *Groany Joni*.

3. Blindfold player, turn them around twice (to make them dizzy), then point them in the direction of the posters. Player tries to pin or tape the card on the chosen poster to win a point. If they hit the spot, **they** earn a point for their team. Place card on the right side before the next player takes their turn. The team with the most pin-up points wins!

### Choosing the Best Me (Goal Chart)

1. Obtain, color, and cut out the *Choosing the Best Me Goal Chart* (shown right).
2. Talk and learn about the nutrition and health, grooming and modesty goals.
Write your goals (things you want to improve) on the chart to remind you to make good choices.

↓ Cut carefully along the inside of the dotted line.

Groan! Joh!

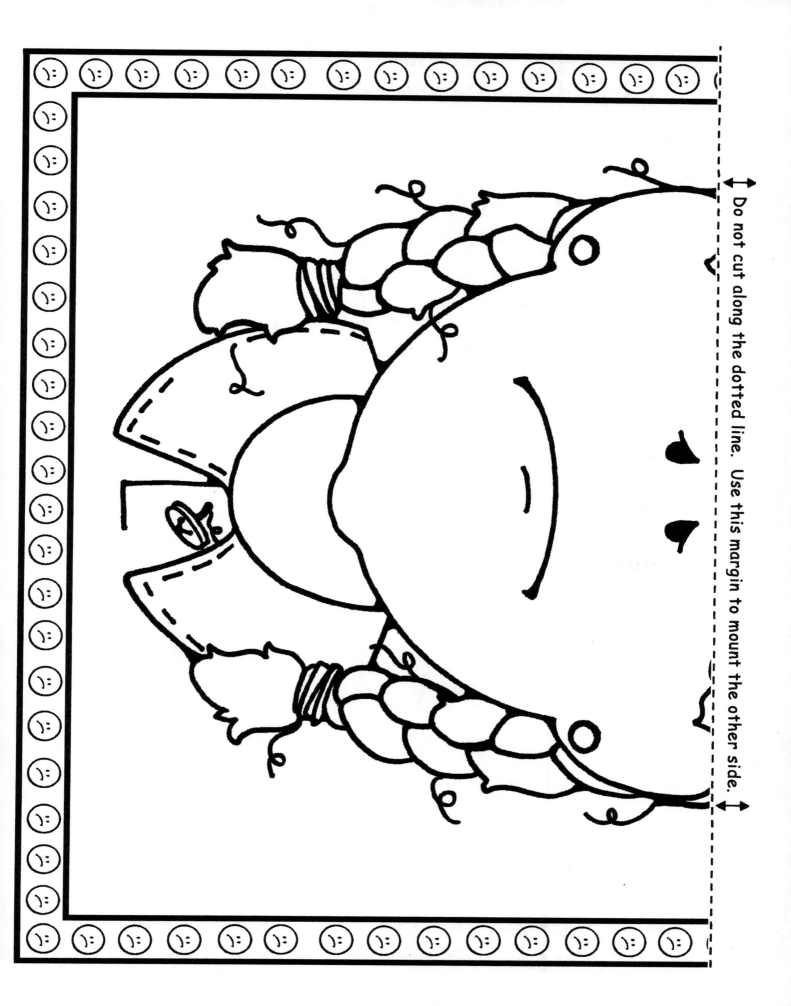

Do not cut along the dotted line. Use this margin to mount the other side.

Cut carefully along the inside of the dotted line.

Glowy Cloe

Do not cut along the dotted line. Use this margin to mount the other side.

I get the sleep I need every night and wake up refreshed.

I enjoy many types of exercise and I feel stronger when I work out.

I like eating meals that that are healthy and I eat only what I need.

I drink plenty of water and it refreshes and cleanses my body.

I keep my hair and skin clean and I feel better when I have showered daily.

I keep my body free of tattoos and body piercings because my body is special.

I wash my hands regularly and keep my nails clean and attractive.

I love having a hairstyle that is attractive and easy to care for.

My clothes are clean and comfortable.

My skirts and my shorts are not too short. I can still be modest and in style.

My shirts are not too short or too low cut. I feel secure when I am modest.

I know my Heavenly Father cares about me and wants me to care for and protect my body.

I stay up late because I'd rather watch TV than spend time sleeping.

Exercise makes me sweat and it takes too long to get results, so I don't worry about it.

I like all kinds of food, especially fast food, and I could never give up sugary treats!

Water is so boring. I'd rather have a soda pop.

I shower to clean my hair and skin, but sometimes I can go without showering for three days!

Tattoos and body piercings are the in thing! My friends are all getting them.

Washing your hands is overrated. There aren't that many germs to worry about.

It's too much trouble to wash my hair more than once a week.

I like tight clothes. All the movie stars wear them.

Short skirts and shorts are all I can find at the stores.

I like my shirts with low necklines. They may be a bit revealing, but all the girls wear them.

I have heard that we should respect our bodies, but that seems so old-fashioned.

# I Can Make Good Choices For My Body

I want that happy, healthy glow that caring for myself will bring.

I will improve my
nutrition by:

_____

_____

I will improve my
grooming by:

_____

_____

I will improve my
health by:

_____

_____

I will improve my
modesty by:

_____

_____

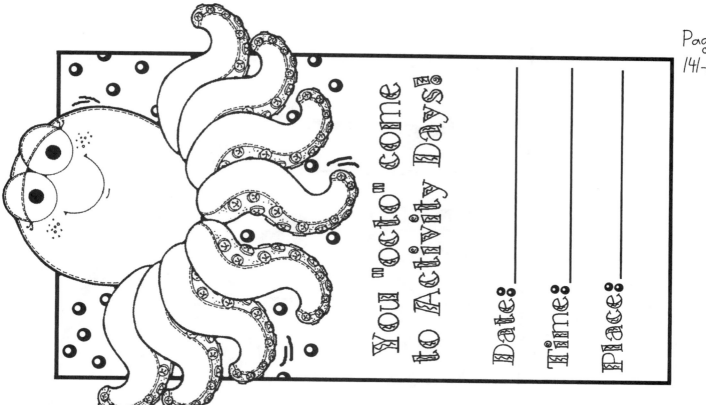

You "octo" come
to Activity Days©

Date::
Time::
Place::

## Developing Talents   Goal 10

**ACTIVITY:** *Plan and complete your own activity that will help you develop your talents.   Write the activity on the octopus (detailed below).*

### Arm Yourself with Talents (Talented Octopus)

1. Obtain, color, and cut out the  *Talented Octopus* (shown right).

2. Reach out and arm yourself with talents using the *Talented Octopus*. Tape the octopus body on your mirror with the arms below. Write things you want to do to develop your talents on the octopus arms. When you have completed the task on the arm, attach the arm to the octopus (arming your octopus, making her strong). This way you can truly serve others.

## Talents: I Will Develop My Talents

*Talent Ideas:* Some say they need to be born with talents, but most people decide they want to do something and work to achieve that talent. What do you want to do that will benefit yourself and others? Here are some talents and gifts that you may want to develop:  sports • drawing  • music • auto mechanics • hairstyling • homemaking • cooking • sewing • gardening • babysitting • writing fiction or nonfiction • mending • painting • pet care • writing music • pet grooming • dancing • horse training • carpentry • scrapbooking • giving parties • singing • gymnastics • jewelry making • dancing • crafts

*Personality Talents:*  caring • charming • cooperative • considerate • creative • decisive • efficient • encouraging • enthusiastic • faithful • forgiving • giving • good example • healthy • intelligent • listener • love unconditionally (not pass judgement) • peacemaker • pleasant • prompt • self-motivated • sense of humor • sharing • sociable • supportive • sympathetic • tactful • talkative • thoughtful • unselfish • understanding

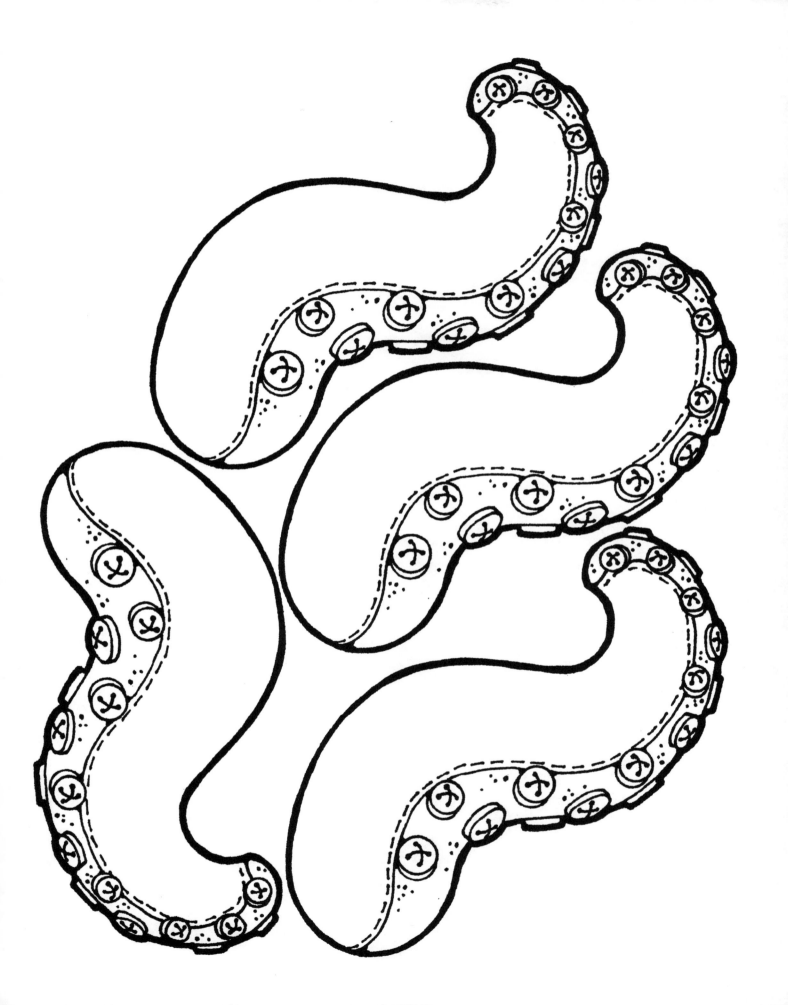

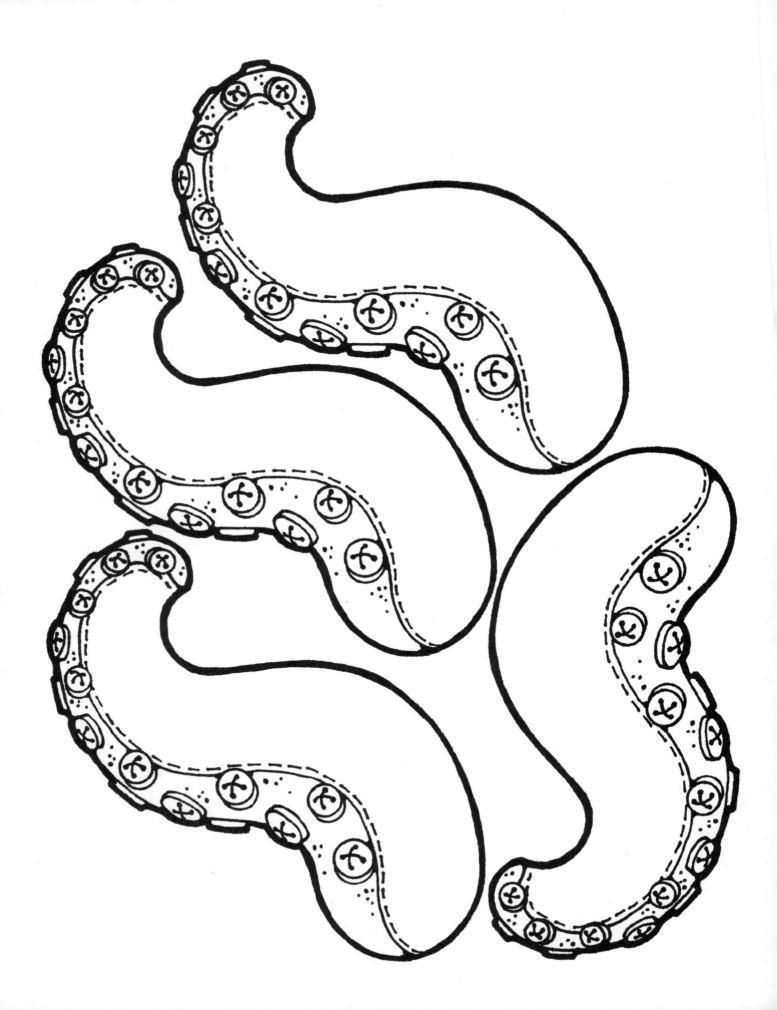

## 1. BUDGETING: I Will Pay Tithing and Save My Money

(Tithing Toast). Cut a piece of toast in half (remove crust) to create bills. Cut round coin shapes with a bottle lid. Place toast bill and 10 toast coins in a clear zip-close bag.

**To Make Money Toast:** Butter bread and sprinkle colored sugar (green for bills and yellow for coins. To color sugar, add food coloring to granulated sugar and mix in a plastic zip-close bag). Broil buttered and sugared toast 2-3 minutes in the oven. **Thought:** Tell children that they might become "toast" in the latter days, when the earth is cleansed by fire, if they do not pay their tithing. Read the following scriptures: D&C 64:23— *"He that is tithed shall not be burned at his coming,"* and D&C 85:3— *"He may tithe his people, to prepare them against the day of vengeance and burning."*

## 2. TALENTS: I Will Prepare to Serve Others

(Stretching Talents String Licorice Game). Purchase two packages of string licorice (for 10 girls) and play this fun game to brainstorm community-service ideas.

**To Create Game:** Write up a list of 15-20 service ideas, e.g., talents we can develop that help us serve (see goal activity, or check the Community Service column in local newspaper, or check with library for ideas). On each of the 15 separate slips of paper, write the numbers 1, 2, 3, 4, or 5. Cut out and fold all service ideas and numbers in the same container and mix together.

**To Play:** (1) Divide into two teams. Have teams take turns drawing a wordstrip or number from the container. (2) If they draw a service idea, they tell how they might perform this community service. Then collect one string of licorice for their team. (3) If they draw a number, e.g., "5," name five service projects needed in a community within 30 seconds and collect 5 strings of licorice for their team. (3)The team with the most licorice strings wins. *Option:* Tie licorice strings together. Measure at the end to see who has the longest string. Say, "We will go the extra mile to serve in our community."

**Thought:** Ask girls to stretch the piece of licorice and think about stretching their talents as they serve.

## 3. WRITING: I Can Teach Gospel Principles

(Cinch-by-the-Inch Wafer Cookies). Provide three wafer cookies and a tube of frosting for each girl. Have them write the letter "C" on the first wafer, "B" on the second wafer, and "I" on the third wafer. Mark the wafers along the sides like a ruler, showing the inch, quarter-inch, half-inch, and three-fourth-inch marks (using short lines like a ruler).

**Thought:** Tell girls that we can learn as we teach others that living the gospel is a "cinch-by-the-inch." As we live the gospel principles each day we can stay on the strait and narrow path which will lead us back to our heavenly home.

## 4. CRAFTS: I Can Create Many Works of Art

(Nature Hike Trail Mix). Go on a nature hike and take along some trail mix by combining and packaging nuts, dried fruit, crackers, carob or chocolate chips, and more.

## 5. CULTURAL ARTS: I Will Learn to Appreciate the Arts

(Self-Portrait Cookies). Roll out and cut out sugar-cookie dough into a 5" x 6" square. Using cookie paints (2 drops of food coloring in 2 tablespoons of canned milk), paint a self-portrait and bake.

## 6. EDUCATION: I Will Improve My Study Habits

(Honey "Bee" Smart Taffy). Make honey taffy (recipe below) and share with girls. **Thought:** Suggest they work hard to get an education so they can be better mothers and provide for their families if they need to. Tell them, "We can follow the example of the busy bees who work all day carrying the pollen and nectar from the flowers to their hive. Let's 'bee' smart and work hard."

**To Make Honey Taffy:** The girls can help make this quick-and-easy honey taffy. In a medium-sized saucepan, bring to boil 1 cup of honey, boiling honey 7-10 minutes on medium high heat, cooking to a soft-ball stage. Test by dropping 1/2 teaspoon honey into cold water. If you can form it into a round ball it's done. Pour onto a buttered surface, e.g., a marble or plastic cutting board, and cool 5 minutes. Then pull and stretch it into taffy, adding butter as you pull. Roll and cut into bite-size pieces to eat.

## 7. HOMEMAKING: I Will Learn to Help at Home

(Beat the Clock Cookies). Create a clock cookie by frosting a round sugar cookie with numbers and two clock hands. **Thought:** Tell girls their hands are needed to make their homes beautiful places to live. Remind them it only takes five minutes a day on each task to develop their talents as homemakers.

## 8. PHYSICAL FITNESS: I Will Develop Strength

("Spread Your Wings" Butterfly Snack). Spread peanut butter in center of a 4" piece of celery. Press cheese triangles into the peanut butter. Add pretzel antennas and raisin eyes. **Thought:** As you eat, think of ways you want to spread your wings, developing physical strength.

## 9. CHOICES: I Will Make Good Choices for My Body

(Silhouette Sandwich). Out of two pieces of bread, carve a girl's silhouette. Mix half butter and half honey together and spread mixture inside to make a sandwich. **Thought:** Tell girls that making good choices for their bodies—taking care of their health and appearance—is "sweet."

## 10. TALENTS: I Will Develop My Talents

(Your Favorite Recipes). Have a tasting table where girls can bring prepared food and share their favorite recipes. **Thought:** Tell girls that to learn to cook they have to invest the time necessary to learn various recipes. As with any other talent, the results are worth the effort. Remind them to "cook up a storm, but don't let the dishes *reign*"—cleaning as they go, so when they serve the meal, the dirty cooking dishes are already done.

We need you at Activity Days!

Date: _____

Time: _____

Place: _____

Preparing for Young Women
Goals 1-5

ACTIVITY: *Complete the following activities while you are 11 years old. They will help you prepare to become a righteous young woman and to participate in the Young Women Personal Progress program. Read D&C 87:8.*

Plan and Prepare for Young Women (Planner Forms)

1. Obtain and color the five planner forms (shown right).
2. Fill in the forms as you complete the activities.

# Seek Uplifting and Virtuous Things

### Preparing for Young Women — Goal 1:

After studying the thirteenth article of faith, make a list of things that are uplifting and virtuous, as follows:

_____

_____

_____

_____

_____

_____

Discuss with a parent or leader how you can seek after these things. Discussion Ideas:

_____

_____

_____

_____

_____

_____

_____

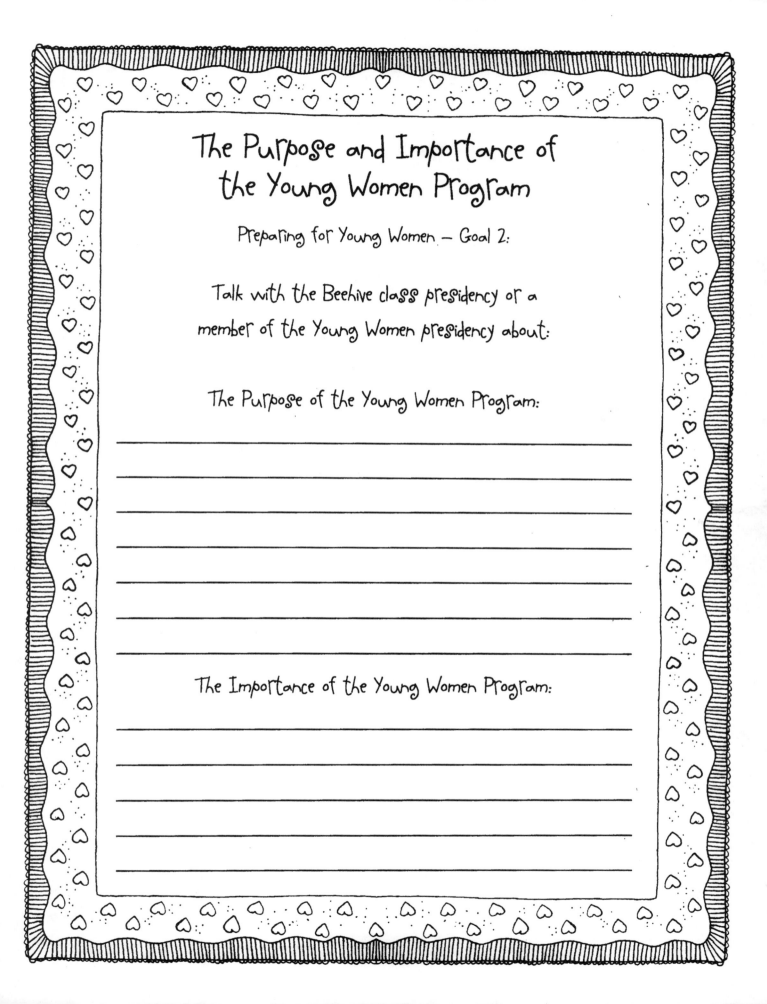

# The Purpose and Importance of the Young Women Program

Preparing for Young Women — Goal 2:

Talk with the Beehive class presidency or a member of the Young Women presidency about:

The Purpose of the Young Women Program:

_____

_____

_____

_____

_____

_____

The Importance of the Young Women Program:

_____

_____

_____

_____

_____

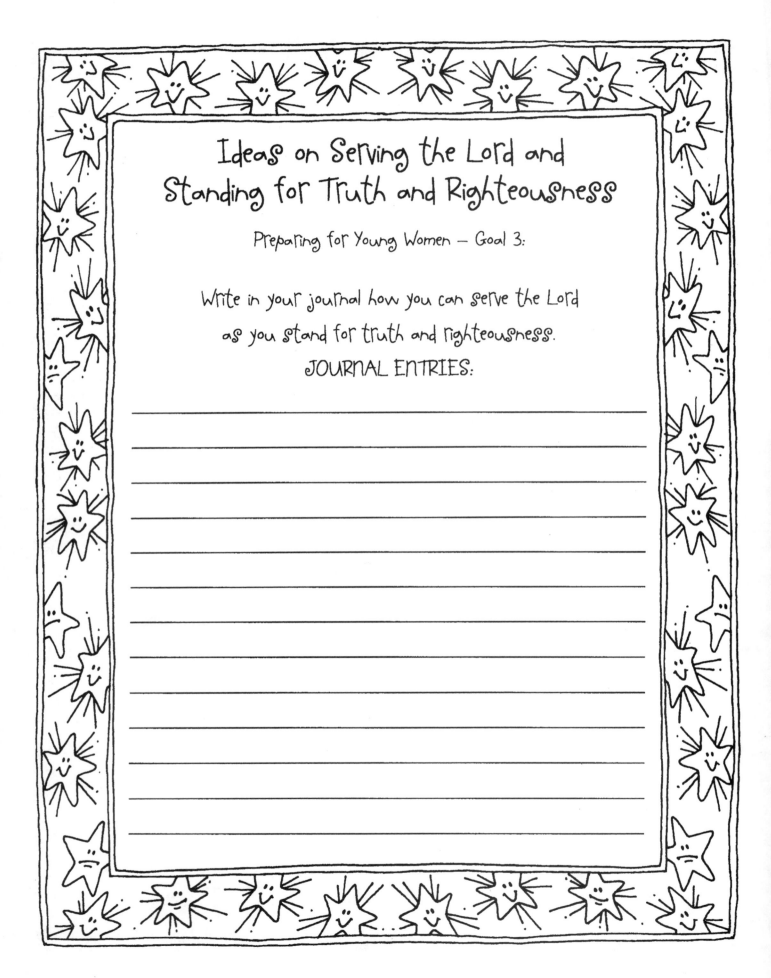

# Ideas on Serving the Lord and Standing for Truth and Righteousness

Preparing for Young Women – Goal 3:

Write in your journal how you can serve the Lord
as you stand for truth and righteousness.

JOURNAL ENTRIES:

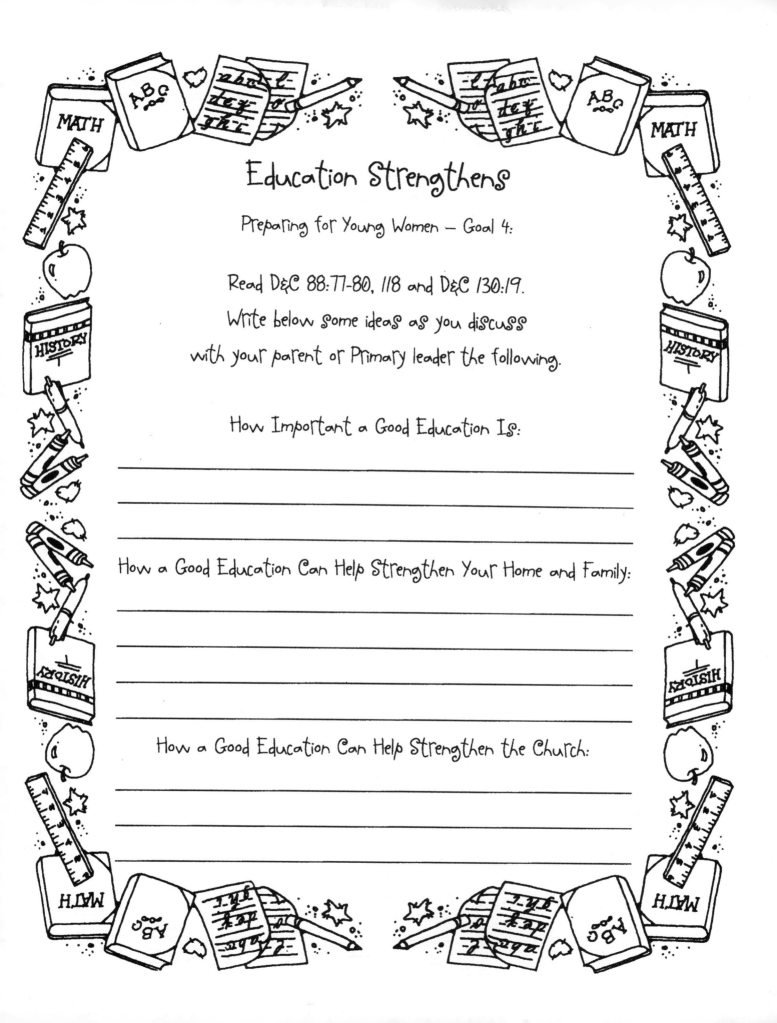

# Education Strengthens

Preparing for Young Women — Goal 4:

Read D&C 88:77-80, 118 and D&C 130:19.
Write below some ideas as you discuss
with your parent or Primary leader the following.

How Important a Good Education Is:

_____

_____

_____

How a Good Education Can Help Strengthen Your Home and Family:

_____

_____

_____

_____

How a Good Education Can Help Strengthen the Church:

_____

_____

_____

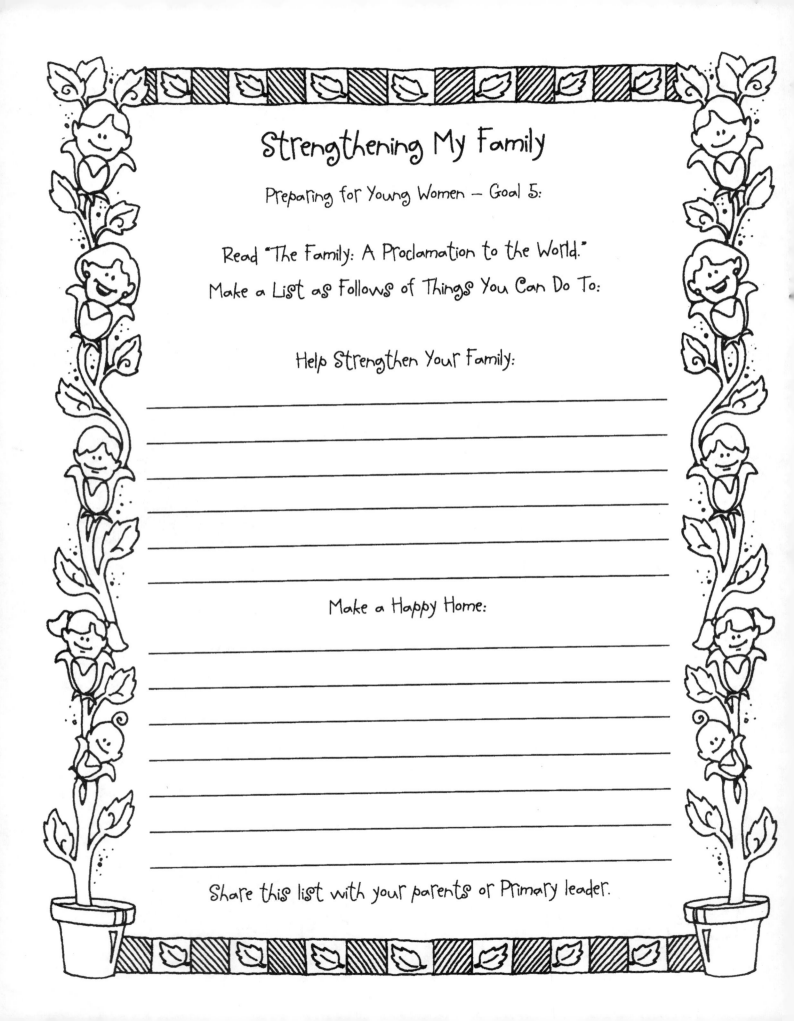

# Strengthening My Family

Preparing for Young Women — Goal 5:

Read "The Family: A Proclamation to the World."

Make a List as Follows of Things You Can Do To:

Help Strengthen Your Family:

_____

_____

_____

_____

_____

_____

Make a Happy Home:

_____

_____

_____

_____

_____

_____

Share this list with your parents or Primary leader.

# Enjoy Full-Color, Ready-to-Use Activities
## Preview of
# Gospel Fun Activities

## Quick-and-Easy Family Home Evenings and Sharing Time

In minutes you can teach a child basic principles of the gospel from the post-and-present games and activities in this book. Because a picture is worth 1,000 words, we have created the visuals that will help you teach the gospel with very little effort. These teaching tools are easy to present by mounting them on a poster, board, or wall.  Children enjoy creating and presenting the activities, so put them in charge whenever you can.

These *Gospel Fun Activities* are ideal for family home evening and Primary sharing time. Parents can use the activities and thought treats to simplify family home evening lessons and make learning fun.  Primary leaders and teachers can use the ideas to create sharing time presentations and add to lessons.

The visuals are ready-to-use to post and present, helping you teach the following gospel subjects:

- Accountability
- Choose the Right
- Commandments
- Faith
- Follow Jesus
- The Holy Ghost
- Missionary Talents
- Missionary Work
- Repentance
- Second Coming
- Service
- Testimony

# Enjoy Full-Color, Ready-to-Use Learning Activities

## Preview of Gospel Games Fun Activities for Family Home Evening and Primary

Use these 37 easy learning games to teach principles of the gospel in family home evening, Primary or Sunday School lessons, or Primary sharing time.

The good times will roll on week after week as you get children, teens, and parents involved in these anytime fun games. Children enjoy creating and presenting the activities, so put them in charge whenever you can.

Although this book is in full color and ready to use, the games are also available to print (the visuals) from CD-ROM in color or black and white.

You'll find such games as:

- Articles of Faith: Thirteen Lucky Numbers
- BEARS: Be Enthusiastic About Reading Scriptures
- Choices Thumbs Up, Thumbs Down
- Commandments Testimony Toss
- Cooperation: Love at Home Spin-the-Bottle
- Education: School is Cool! Match Game
- Honesty Pays Blessings Bucks
- Invite the Spirit Choices Game
- Love Lingo Bingo
- Preparing for Life's Mission
- Priesthood Power Ponder
- Righteous Example Drama or Draw
- Second Coming Millennium Match Game
- Standard Works—Scripture Think-a-thon
- Turn Trials into Triumphs Match Game
- Valiant Testimony Board Game
  and more.

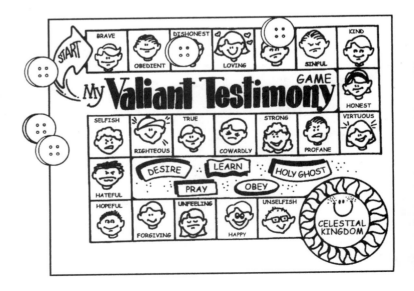